BALANCED LIVES
Changing work patterns for men

NEW WAYS TO WORK

1995

Contents

Index to case histories

Acknowledgements

I think that flexible working is extremely beneficial for my relationship with my children at a key stage in their development, but is a bad move, temporarily, for my career. Obviously I have struck a good bargain.

Divisional Deputy Director, University

We would like to thank NatWest who have generously sponsored *Balanced Lives: Changing work patterns for men.*

A project on the scale of *Balanced Lives* could not have happened without the good will of the many supporters and friends of New Ways to Work.

We would like to thank Richard Bainbridge, Tony Cornah, and Sarosh Dastur who were so generous with their time in helping to pilot the questionnaire.

Gill Forster, Senior Lecturer in Human Resource Management at Newcastle Business School, University of Northumbria carried out a preliminary investigation and literature research which informed the development of this project.

Michel Syrett, a member of the Advisory Panel at New Ways to Work, kindly read the first draft and his expertise has been essential.

We are grateful to Gill Forster, Jenny Hurstfield and June Saltmarsh for conducting detailed interviews and assisting with the case studies.

And finally we would like to thank the men who replied so fully to our questionnaire, those who gave their time to be interviewed and to those men who wrote to New Ways to Work thanking us for giving them a long needed 'voice' to express their views about work and life issues.

Preface

I enjoy Milton, though one of his most quoted lines: 'They also serve who only stand and wait' has always irritated me. Of course Milton was making a more profound point, but the words are often casually used to justify what the French call an 'acte de presence' – just being there, not *doing* anything other than fulfilling an obligation to remain on the premises, as if that were the best proof of one's commitment to the organisation.

Cary Cooper has coined the word 'presenteeism' to describe this pernicious practice. (Since he, like me, has spent many hours vainly watching Manchester City attempt to play football, he knows what he is talking about.)

The pressure of long hours on men is a serious problem, with insidious effects on family life. I have lived those problems myself.

The answer is simple enough, you may think: just go home. But to men under pressure at work that is not useful advice. More sophisticated strategies are needed to reconcile the often conflicting demands of work and family life.

Little research has been done so far on how those strategies can best be developed, which is why this book is particularly welcome now. Working from case studies it shows just how complex the problem is, and how much it has worsened in recent years. It also teases out practical solutions which men have begun to devise for themselves.

I am, frankly, a sceptic about the potential for useful government intervention. What is most important is for employers to accept, as Rover have done, that 'helping people achieve a balanced home life is the surest way of increasing their contribution to the company'.

If this study prompts just one more company to accept that message and act on it, it will have been worthwhile.

Howard Davies
Director- General, Confederation of British Industry (CBI)

Foreword

There are a number of drivers for change in the 1990s including advances in technology, increasing globalisation, and changing consumer expectations which heighten competition and need a new approach to balance effectively the conflicting demands which arise.

NatWest is responding to these challenges by recognising and valuing the diversity of all of our stakeholders, including staff, customers and suppliers. Our inter-relationships with our people provide the key to our success.

One of the ways in which we can recognise and manage the different needs of our staff, is to increase the range of opportunities for working flexibly; enabling staff to work in new and innovative ways, meeting their lifestyle demands, while matching the demands of our customers and business.

NatWest pioneered the introduction of Career Break Schemes during the early 1980s and the range of flexible leave schemes have continued to evolve, recognising the different and changing needs of our workforce. However flexible working opportunities have traditionally appealed to (*and been taken up by*) women for a variety of reasons.

In the UK, we are witnessing a major change in family dynamics, for example the growth of dual career families, single parent families, heightened childcare expectations and an increase in caring roles for elderly relatives. There is a growing desire for more leisure time and a 'balance' between working and non-working lives, caring responsibilities are being shared more equally between men and women.

These changes have a marked effect upon the traditional approaches to flexible working, challenging assumptions and stereotypes about the role of men and women in the workplace and at home.

NatWest is therefore delighted to support the production of *Balanced Lives*, which aims to help change perceptions, attitudes and expectations. It is designed to help employers develop more innovative and flexible employment practices and contains examples and case studies about men from a variety of backgrounds, who are already balancing their lives successfully.

Martin Gray

Martin Gray
Chief Executive, NatWest UK

BALANCED LIVES:
Changing work patterns for men
A summary

Changing the balance

Over recent years it has largely been women who have demanded and made use of flexible work patterns. They have made significant progress in creating a different balance between work and home life. However, there has been a hidden assumption that family friendly means women friendly. What about men?

Balanced Lives: Changing work patterns for men draws from the views and experiences of 106 men who returned questionnaires to New Ways to Work early in 1995. Seventeen were interviewed in depth and their case histories are included. The men surveyed are working reduced and flexible hours, taking career breaks and working from home in a variety of roles and settings. *Balanced Lives* outlines why men are working flexibly, how they negotiated their arrangement, the attitudes of colleagues and senior staff and the effect of organisational culture. It also examines the role of paternity, parental and family leave and draws from experiences in other countries.

The opportunity to lead a balanced, quality life was a high priority for the men surveyed. For many the opportunity for more flexibility, in the working week, year and over their working lifetime gives them time:

- to spend with their families and friends
- to be involved in community activities, ranging from being a lay preacher to serving meals on wheels
- to study and carry out research
- to follow leisure interests such as mountaineering, travel, gardening and to develop freelance art work

Men who are working flexibly have increased motivation and energy. This is positive for both them and their employers. We now need a different measure of commitment at work which considers an individual's output rather than just the visible time they spend in the workplace.

Many men feel under psychological pressure to work long hours. In the current economic climate it is hard to challenge this. Workloads for managers have increased such that in a survey one in five said their workload had increased by more than 15 hours a week in just two years. In this context there is an urgent need to question whether employees can really accomplish more effective and quality work in long hours. Some organisations are already beginning to confront this issue. Stressed employees are bad for business, leading to increased absenteeism as well as low productivity.

There is a need for changing attitudes and behaviour towards those who opt to work more flexibly. An organisational culture which positively values people's lives outside the workplace will improve the situation. In addition the conventional view of careers and career development needs examination.

Although policies on flexible working have largely been targeted at women, men are beginning to make use of these options, with a resultant positive effect on the balance of their lives. Positive role models, as those presented in this book, will help encourage both men and their employers to make working flexibly a real choice for more men.

Reducing hours worked has financial implications for both pay and pensions. The vast majority of men surveyed were in professional well paid jobs, where the choice to opt for reduced pay is a real option. However, a number of men were in semi skilled jobs with lower pay levels, but they still chose quality of life over higher pay. There is an urgent need for pension systems to be reviewed to take into account the diversity of working arrangements now in operation.

Paternity leave, parental leave and family leave are options which increasingly men consider to be important. In other European countries these options are more widespread.

Achieving change

For men: think laterally and flexibly. You may be surprised to find that your proposal to work reduced or more flexible arrangements is easier to negotiate than you thought. Flexible employment is needed to meet the changing demands of customers. Your ability to balance customers' needs with your own requirements will strengthen your case.

For organisations: Recognise that long hours and stressed employees do not result in high quality, effective outputs. Create a healthier working environment which provides opportunities for flexibility and for your employees to lead more balanced lives.

For Government: Provide a legal framework which acknowledges that both men and women have an equally important role to play in caring responsibilities, for example by establishing a right to a minimum of five days statutory paternity leave and family leave.

For society: What happened to the so-called leisure society so talked about 20 years ago? What happened to the quality of life? Why is the reality that so many people in employment are working longer hours than we were when so many others are unemployed? In the USA the average employee now works the equivalent of an extra month each year compared to 1969. It is time to change the balance. It is healthier for society, healthier for business and healthier for us all, now and in the future.

Chapter one: Introduction

The quiet revolution

Traditional balances in the workplace are changing.

Against a backdrop of economic, social and technological change, employers are recognising that professionalism, flexibility and innovation are key attributes required in the workplace to remain competitive in the 1990s and beyond. Equally employees are seeking more flexibility and choice in order to fulfil their personal commitments.

For some years women have been seeking a better balance between work and home. In many cases it is being acknowledged that a balance can be created between their desire and need to work flexibly and the rapid growth in flexible employment practices to meet more demanding customer needs.

In the past working reduced and flexible hours for women meant taking jobs with low pay and status, and reduced rights and benefits. More recently increasing numbers of women have been successful in obtaining more equitable flexibility. They are working reduced hours and from home with pro rata benefits in a wide range of jobs, including some at senior levels.

Men too, although in small numbers, are seeking flexibility and choice in the way in which they work. A quiet revolution is happening, which is largely unacknowledged by most politicians and social policy makers but is beginning to be recognised by employers.

In order to investigate how and why men are working reduced and flexible hours, taking career breaks and working from home, New Ways to Work decided to undertake a qualitative study of men already working these arrangements (See Appendix for methodology). We received questionnaires from 106 men and 17 in depth case studies were undertaken. *Balanced Lives: Changing Work Patterns For Men* clearly demonstrates that some men are working effectively on a flexible basis in a variety of new and different settings and roles. Although the sample is small, the findings highlight important issues which need addressing if the options are to be available to more men.

"My favourite word is balance and for me it was about weighing up all the aspects of time, money and career opportunities. Working three days a week is the best balance."

The men featured in *Balanced Lives* are displaying flexibility, a genuine enthusiasm for work, increased motivation and a rediscovered creativity, all of which is good news for men and their employers. There is positive evidence that these men are using their valued position in their organisations to seek different ways of working to improve their quality of life. With less pressure to be the sole provider in the family, men are realising that they can have a choice too.

Encouraging the pursuit of well balanced lives among employees will ensure that organisations maximise the contributions of all their staff – men as well as women.

"Helping people achieve a balanced home life is the surest way of increasing their contribution to the company."
Rover Group

So why are there so few men changing their work patterns at a time when there are many sound reasons for men as well as women to consider change?

Men and the business case

For a start, there are strong business reasons for flexible employment practices.

Employers of the 1990s are openly recognising that in order to achieve lasting competitive advantage they need to value and respect the diversity of both their customers and employees. They are recognising that people are central to their success and are acknowledging that effective use of flexible employment at all levels for both men and women can maximise contributions to their organisations by acknowledging individual differences and matching individual needs and preferences to changing business requirements.

More and more, employers are producing flexible employment policies and practices which are proving to be more responsive to the fast changing competitive climate and diverse cultures within which they operate than more conventional, and often inflexible, working patterns.

For businesses whose customers are expecting a service up to 24 hours a day and seven days a week flexible working provides a cost-effective solution. Flexible employment practices provide opportunities for more creative organisational development to meet changing business needs while helping reduce staff turnover, attract and retain good quality staff with valued and relevant skills, reduce training costs and increase productivity.

All these factors have a positive effect on profitability as well as the added bonus of providing employees with opportunities for flexibility and the ability to balance their work and personal commitments. It makes sound business sense for men as well as women to benefit as some men who gave us their views are beginning to realise:

"Although my type of role is unusual, I think it shows that the organisation is changing, probably because it was seen as cost effective to do so."

"I'm in the fortunate position that I'm seen as a valuable asset to the organisation. They wouldn't want to lose me. The Chief Executive (who I report to) said we hire you for your brains not the number of hours you sit in an office."

"I would like to improve the organisation's image and its understanding of farming matters, particularly at branch level. During my career, I have built up a sound understanding of farms' financial needs. I understand the industry and I can talk easily with farmers and gain their confidence. If I had retired naturally – ie age 60, the package I obtained (to work from home on an hourly consultant basis) would not then have been on offer. Therefore the opportunity to work on specialist farm financial cases seemed to me to be the best of all worlds. Doing something I really enjoy, without all the day to day hassle."

The compatibility of work and family life is becoming a strategic challenge for organisations in the 1990s together with the recognition of mutual benefits to both employers and employees alike. Price Waterhouse for example is changing its culture to create a climate where employees' needs can be fulfilled. This includes in house workshops for fathers, short term flexible leave arrangements for men and women and more encouragement for all staff to take their full holiday entitlements.

Rodger O'Connell, an independent Management Consultant and Trainer, has also explored some of the potential benefits of fatherhood for the employer, for example better time management, multi-tasking, coaching, more adaptability, improved listening and negotiating skills, and more informed decision-making. These are all valued qualities for managers in the 1990s and they emphasise the positive advantages of fatherhood to businesses.

The business reasons for men to change their working patterns are compelling. However, there are other equally important reasons why men should consider change.

Men, long hours and stress

Questioning the need for long hours

"The old work ethos of long hours may have worked where most wives stayed at home, but the long term effects of 'presenteeism' on families where both partners work will be ill health and less effective performances when they are at work."

Professor Cary Cooper

Many men (and women) are working longer hours as a result of operational restructuring and delayering. Larger workloads are being managed by fewer staff and heightened competition both between and within organisations, has increased the pressures of work. While parts of the workforce are unemployed or underemployed, others are working longer hours than ever before. Increasingly, an individual's working life is being concentrated into 25 or 30 years, between the ages of 20 and 50, as people enter the workforce later and leave earlier.

It is clear that many men feel under psychological pressure to work long hours. One man working in a large company commented: *"There are entrenched views of commitment (demonstrated by physical presence, usually long hours). Few men are willing to challenge this in the current uncertain economic conditions."*

Professor Cary Cooper, an organisational psychologist and Pro Vice Chancellor of the University of Manchester Institute for Science and Technology (UMIST), has coined the term 'presenteeism'. This is the exact opposite to absenteeism – being at work when you should be at home, either because you are ill, or because you are working such long hours that you are no longer effective. He believes that the motivation for working such excessive hours is fear, a way of visibly demonstrating commitment to the company.

This is borne out by statistical data. British people work the longest average working week in Europe. Sixteen per cent work more than 48 hours a week and three out of four British men work 40 plus hours a week compared to the European average of one in four. Almost 50 per cent of the British workforce report coming home feeling totally exhausted, compared with 36 per cent in America and 17 per cent in Holland.

However, two-thirds of those working long hours want to work shorter hours. Ideally 30 per cent of all employees would like to work 30 hours or less and a fifth under 20 hours. Fourteen per cent of men want to work less than 30 hours a week compared with 53 per cent of women, although only three per cent of men and 44 per cent of women already work part time.

These figures (from a 1995 Trades Union Congress survey and the European Commission) illustrate that men are beginning to question the long hours culture and challenge its long term effects upon their future.

Working round the clock

One of the reasons why long hours are worked, particularly by men, is that traditionally they have accompanied career success, especially at senior levels. Change then becomes difficult as long hours are seen as the norm and are used as a measure of commitment. Any reduction of working hours therefore has been seen as a reduction in commitment to the organisation.

Yet how productive are long hours? A manager from the private sector commented:

"I think there is a long hours culture, but my answer to this is, if you are working 50-60 hours a week, how many are really productive? It's human nature, that you just cannot be productive for long periods of time. I also know that a lot of it is about playing games. I remember working with a manager who said that he was frightened to go before his boss went, so he used to have an office that overlooked the car park and he would stay in his office all the time his boss's car was there. He would just sit at his desk, and wait."

The real focus should be on quality, effectiveness and meeting objectives, both individually and through teamwork. This would replace the outdated loyalty to time and place which ceases to be realistic as a more diverse range of working patterns is needed to satisfy customer and employee demands.

A study of working patterns of top National Health Service managers in 1994 found that the average working week was 56 hours and 43 per cent worked over 60 hours per week. All top managers work long hours irrespective of their personal and domestic circumstances. A recent Institute of Management study of 1,250 managers found that eight out of ten were working more than six hours in excess of their official working week. 'Presenteeism' can be taken to the point of absurdity where flexibility has come to mean working around the clock, attending breakfast meetings, taking work home in the evenings and at weekends.

Changing traditional assumptions

The time has come to challenge traditional assumptions.

In her book *Breaking the Mold: Women, men and time in the new corporate world*, Lotte Bailyn, Professor of Management at the Massachusetts Institute of Technology asks *"Why are professional employees expected to work such long hours? Can one really accom-*

plish more in twelve hours than in ten, or eight? Some evidence clearly indicates that the answer is no. And why is visibility – presence at the workplace – such a critical indicator of commitment? Many tasks, particularly those that require careful thought and attention, are accomplished better and more easily away from an office."

More than anything else, there is a need to re-examine the assumptions we have about the role of time in the evaluation and development of high level careers. For too long it has been assumed that long hours equate with productivity, an assumption anchored in assembly line work.

However, in other spheres of work, long hours can be viewed as a sign of inefficiency rather than as an indicator of commitment and performance. A male solicitor measures performance differently:

"The starting point is for firms to realise that if people are working very long extended hours the quality of their work towards the end of the working week must deteriorate because they're tired. The quality of decision making must suffer. You expand to fit the time so you're not necessarily doing more work, you're just taking longer to do it. You're not being effective or managing time. If you turn the argument on its head you might say you'll get more productive work from people who are fresher, more focused and more organised. There are positive benefits to any organisation in a low hours culture instead of a long hours culture. Then it becomes obvious that a job share fits into that scheme of things. In my view our firm benefits greatly from the fact that both of us work short hours. We make them up to a total but we are definitely fresher, more focused and harder working for the hours we are there."

In this era of high speed communications and information technology, 'face time', visible time at work is also no longer a valid basis for the judgement of high performance. A man working for a multinational corporation describes the effect of increasing globalisation where the work day is in fact 24 hours a day: *"We use an electronic mail system which is very powerful and goes all around the world. So particularly, if you are dealing with America, they don't wake up till our lunch time, and if you are dealing with the West Coast, Alaska, then it's even later, they are not in work till 5 o'clock our time."*

Time is money
Last year, Caroline Slocock, Head of Treasury Personnel Policy, HM Treasury, put the issue of long hours firmly onto the agenda and a year into the project has cited 'modest improvements.'

It was women, not men, who identified long hours as a key problem. However, opinions were divided within the Treasury as there were those who believed long hours were necessary. A project team was established which addressed issues around long hours, especially after 25 per cent of senior people were made redundant. A survey of work areas concluded that 90 per cent felt the culture at the Treasury was one of long hours and 80 per cent said that effectiveness and motivation were affected. It was also seen as a particular issue for parents of younger children. The survey indicated that staff at different levels worked on average three (at the lowest levels) and 27 (at the highest levels) extra hours, with middle to senior managers working around 15 extra hours over the standard work week.

The Treasury has defined long hours as excess hours, ie long hours over a period of time and not the extra hours needed to match peaks of work. Long hours mainly affect middle to senior managers. Some junior staff felt threatened by the project as they, unlike their senior colleagues, are entitled to overtime payments and had grown accustomed to the income.

Underlying issues concerning time and quality were identified. Searching for ways to save time and better control of overtime led to staff being sent on time management courses. Revised appraisal systems will reflect such issues.

Changes at the Treasury include cutting some areas of work and fewer late meetings. The ministerial box deadline is now 4:00 p.m. instead of much later in the evening. Some changes in culture have been noted including the fact that a man who does not wish to work long hours is no longer considered eccentric. The issue is seen as one of effectiveness and Caroline Slocock emphasised that support from the top was important along with senior managers actually putting policy into practice.

Stress is bad for business

"So I do think there is a kind of a culture which has crept in, I'm sure it's common across British industry. A lot of people here do work very long hours and have stress related illnesses. A lot have been off with breakdowns and a lot of people are questioning their life style. I know it's not just here, it's everywhere. I'm quite clear about what's important to me, and I take the view that I'm going to come here and I'll give it my best when I'm here but then I want to go home, because there are other things in life as well. I think it's up to the individual. One of the problems is that people are unable to say, 'I'm sorry but I can't do this, it's just too much'. That's perceived as weak and feeble."
Manager, private sector

Occupational stress is not good for business. According to the International Labour Office the effects of stress at work are thought to cost up to 10 per cent of Gross National Product in Britain. The Health and Safety Executive estimate that 40 million days per year are lost in the UK due to stress related illness.

Defining stress is very complex. If stress is intense, continuous or repeated, if the person is unable to cope or if support is lacking, then stress can lead to physical illness and psychological disorders. These can range from chronic fatigue to depression, as well as insomnia, anxiety, migraines, emotional upsets, stomach ulcers, allergies, skin disorders, lumbago and rheumatic attacks. And the most serious consequences of all – heart attacks, accidents, and even suicides, may carry penalties for negligent employers.

A duty to care about stress

John Walker was a Social Worker who suffered two nervous breakdowns caused by work stress. He won his claim that his employer, Northumberland County Council had failed in its common law duty of care to provide a safe workplace. Mr. Walker had frequently asked his superiors for more staff and for management guidance, but none was forthcoming. His mental health deteriorated to such an extent that he was unable to return to his 20 year long career. The Court has yet to decide the size of any compensation payment. The public services union UNISON warned that employers who put an unreasonable burden on staff can expect to be taken to court as a result of the High Court ruling.

Research by Cooper and Lewis shows that dual-earner men and women who work in unresponsive, inflexible organisations are more dissatisfied with their jobs and suffer higher levels of stress than those in organisations which respond to their needs for a healthy balance between work and family. Although some men interviewed still experienced stress due to overdemanding jobs, they acknowledged that flexible working meant they had reserves of energy and enthusiasm to tap into. The majority were adamant that working flexibly had a positive effect on their feelings of stress and burnout, including 40 per cent who said the effect was very positive.

Adverse effects on performance and productivity are a high cost for employers to pay. A less stressed, healthy and effective workforce greatly depends on attitudes and policies which allow men and women to lead balanced, productive and rewarding lives.

Recognition that work and family are important is part of the process. A study of very successful and healthy executives of both sexes in the USA in 1990 demonstrated that these were not workaholics, catching only occasional glimpses of their families. Rather they were people who have achieved a healthy balance in their lives, with a satisfying level of involvement in both family and work. In these circumstances stress is normal and necessary.

Working fewer hours, sharing a job and therefore responsibility, or even simply spending less time in traffic as people working from home do, might potentially reduce stress and burnout, by leaving more time for oneself, one's family and for leisure. These factors are pushing men (and women) to challenge the status quo and their traditional assumptions and to seek *Balanced Lives*. The case histories which follow demonstrate how men are quietly doing just that and how they and their employers are reaping the benefits.

Chapter two:
Why men work flexibly

Men and families: changing roles

"The machismo of work is deeply ingrained in the male psyche – God knows why. It's much more interesting to have a varied life and those of us who have opted for a spell of domesticity know our kids far better. May I make the point that some obstacles in the way of men choosing flexible working are internal – it's not all down to intractable employers. Many – I suspect most – men still see themselves as the mighty hunters, going out every day to hunt for dinosaur meat in steamy corporate jungles, whilst the womenfolk nurture the babies and keep the cave warm and tidy. Take that away and they lose a sense of purpose – and more."
Letter from Mike Whitaker to New Ways to Work

Employed fathers work substantially longer hours than employed mothers (42 hours compared to 24 hours a week) according to the British Household Panel Analysis. This is partly because very few fathers work part time. Indeed fathers are less likely to work part time than men in general while mothers are more likely to work part time than women in general. Analysis of the 1991 Labour Force Survey (LFS) shows that one per cent of employed fathers with a child under 10 had a part time job compared to six per cent of all employed men, 44 per cent of all employed women and 69 per cent of women with a child under 10.

A total of 5.4 million employees in Britain worked part time in their main job according to the Spring 1994 Labour Force Survey (LFS). Of these 726,000 (14 per cent) were men. Of the 193,000 part time workers who job share, 11,000 are male (5.7 per cent). Forty-two per cent of male part time employees are students compared with eight per cent of women. Twenty-nine per cent of males work part time because they do not want a full time job, whereas 80 per cent of women worked part time for this reason.

Last year in Holland the FNV (a Dutch Trade Union organisation) launched a special campaign promoting part time work. Colourful posters appeared in the streets and on bus shelters, one of which read simply: 'Hello I'm your daddy.' It needed no further explanation.

Women's earnings continue to make an increasingly important contribution to household budgets, preventing the incomes of thousands of families from falling below poverty levels. According to *Social Policy Research Findings* from a team at the London School of Economics, families headed by a male 'breadwinner' are now outnumbered nearly three to one by homes where both partners work. Married or cohabiting women with part time jobs now typically contribute a fifth of family income and this rises to two-fifths for women who are working full time. Men's contribution to household budgets has fallen to 60 per cent, compared with 75 per cent in the early 1980s.

Although women are working more hours outside the household, their hours of work inside the house have not decreased. The average man working full time spends about 15 hours a week less than his female counterpart on essential activities such as housework, shopping and childcare. A library attendant who is over 60 and works 16.5 hours a week said *"my wife now works full time in a management capacity and therefore we agreed to switch roles".*

In general men and women are cohabiting more, marrying later, becoming parents at older ages and having fewer children. They also divorce more frequently. And fathers in the UK work longer than fathers in any other member state of the EU. The consequent risk to men of losing both partners and children may be leading some men to reconsider their position at work. A man recently wrote to *The Guardian* about his predicament:

"Obtaining job shares is not just a problem for women returning to work after childcare. It is one shared by an increasing number of men. The job of my dreams was mine, but only if I would work full time. Only if I pushed myself out of my children's lives. Only if I reneged on the promise I made to my partner that I would be the prime carer to allow her to follow her career."

Simon Sperryn, Chief Executive of the London Chamber of Commerce, suggested at a seminar in March 1995 for the Working Parents Employer of the Year awards, that ordinary small businesses will not be trendsetters. They will, however be receptive to flexible work policies, because their employees will be affected by demographic changes and elder care. He wondered if there was a new class of family emerging, with both parents working part time and bringing up children together. If his view is correct, the way work is organised and undertaken will need to be constantly reviewed and monitored by employers.

The following case history illustrates how one father involves himself in childcare along with maintaining an active career. Although very busy, he has found balance in playing a full part in family life and relief from being the sole breadwinner.

Colin White works three days a week as a Management Development Specialist for British Telecom:

“ *I work on a development pro-gramme for senior managers which lasts about a year and consists of five specific modules and I'm the manager for one of those modules which is on change management. In the past I was an up front trainer, whereas now I do the design and training. Sue and I have three children, aged six, four and nine months. We had our first baby in 1989 and my wife was on maternity leave for six months. She's a teacher and had negotiated*

a contract to return three days a week and I had my full time job as a Management Trainer. I assumed that I would carry on working full time, because that's what men do. If anybody switches to part time, it's normally the woman. At that time I was also working as a Relate (marriage guidance) Counsellor, so I was very much aware of the pressures that a new baby brings and the pressures that consequently develop when you have the man responsible, as the breadwinner, the sole provider, and if the woman is totally responsible for the child care. This rather traditional set up didn't feel right for us. When Adam was about three months old I was becoming increasingly aware that I wasn't spending enough time with him. I was usually leaving home at half past eight in the morning, and getting home at about six o'clock. By a lot of standards that's excellent, a lot of men would give their right arm for that set up. But I began to think: 'Is there another way, wouldn't it be nice if I could work part time?' So it was a desire on my part to spend more time with Adam and in fairness it was very straightforward to arrange, and I've been doing it ever since.

At that time I worked for someone who was totally career orientated. He lived for work so I thought it was going to be a bit tricky. One day I had a meeting with him and asked if there was any chance of working part time (three days a week)? He was a bit taken aback by this. I did a certain amount of work for him, but I also did work for other groups which was seen as 'outside' work. He said that if I was just to work three days for him he would be quite happy with that. This then freed up a post, so he could get somebody in to do some clerical work, so in fact, it suited him. His boss agreed and referred me to personnel and I found out that although there wasn't a procedure, they were happy as long as line man-agement were. So in September 1989, when Sue went back to work we were both working three days a week and used a childminder for one day. When Matthew was born in 1991,

Sue switched to working two days a week, so that we could cover the whole week between us.

It's a very liberating thing, to know that we both contribute to bringing in the money. It means that if one of us loses our job, for whatever reason, we've still got an income. But overall it's been about balance. I don't feel responsibility as a sole provider, as a lot of men do, and it's been great to have that time with the children, to watch them grow up and to watch those magical moments. It's lovely taking Adam to school, having the time to go to an open assembly and to know what he's talking about.

Being in Personnel, the culture is perhaps different from say an engineering function which might be more traditional in its thinking. I don't think men, by and large know what it's like to be at home. It is very sad that some of the older men that I've spoken to have said, that looking back on it they missed their children growing up because they were working at their career.

I will always be grateful to BT that between us we were able to make this happen and that I was given the time, because once that time has gone, it's gone for ever. I think I've demonstrated that it is possible, certainly in my job, to have that flexibility. I think if leading figures in public life can do it, all the better. For example, Tony Blair takes his children to school. If we can get more and more people in senior positions to do things like that, I think that will bode well for the future. We can all have a more balanced life

In a survey of 1,250 managers published in the *Financial Times* in March 1995 almost half said that although work took priority over everything else in their lives, the majority admitted that they would like to spend more time with family and friends. The survey shows the extent of the extra burden that has fallen on managers during the recession. Workloads for one in five managers had increased by more that 15 hours a week in just two years.

The preliminary research undertaken for this study indicated that men who wanted to work flexibly for personal or career reasons were not seen to be challenging gender expectations, but if they do so for childcare reasons this is seen more negatively. There is a tendency for employers to be more understanding about work/family conflicts for women. Policies regarding flexible working have in reality largely been seen as targeted at women. It is only in more recent years that this is being challenged by the very fact that men are also working on a flexible basis.

Forty three per cent of men who replied to the questionnaire were working on a flexible basis for childcare reasons. A teacher who works three and a half days per week does so to *"create time for children eg taking to school and some time for self"*. A grandfather who is a part time cleaner for a local authority is also a volunteer meals on wheels organiser and *"occasionally cares for grandchildren to allow my daughter to work"*.

Another father proves that managing from a distance is not an obstacle in his post. **Jeremy Spafford** is a Regional Development Manager for Centrepoint, a charity which works to prevent young people from becoming homeless and to assist those who do. He works three days a week on a job share basis and lives in Oxford. His children are nine, seven, and five with another on the way.

> *I was the first person in the organisation ever to be based outside of London so I was being managed from London in a job in Oxford. I was also working part time which was quite unusual for the organisation, and doing the kind of job that was very much out and about. The way I liked to work with the agreement of my manager was that I would work the number of hours I was paid for but would work the hours when they suited me. But there are external constraints. If there are meetings with other people I have to be at those meetings. In so far as I was able to control my time it was down to me, so some days I would work for three hours, other days 10 or 11 hours.*

> *I will be managing eight people once they are in post who will be based in Devon, around Avon, and Warwickshire. What we are doing in Oxfordshire is being replicated in other parts of the country and my job will be to set those up and then supervise them with my job share partner.*

> *I've had to make decisions about not being as involved as I would like to be in the internal workings of the organisation.*

> *It's a really useful thing to be able to carry lots of different agendas. It's been encouraged especially in management and has become a positive thing, instead of a negative thing. Men have been encouraged to try and work like this in a very serious way. I think it's much more interesting.*

A Planning Analyst for a multinational corporation leaves work at 4:30pm most days to collect his children. He finds his colleagues tolerant but irritated at times as *"I leave when they stay"*. However, his colleagues do not see that he also makes up the time. He explains that *"I spend a day at home occasionally – about once every 3/4 weeks. I have a home computer and phone link to office and fax machine. I use my home office evenings and weekends to make up time".*

Eighty per cent of men said that their home life had been positively affected by their flexible working arrangement, including 57 per cent who said the effect was very positive.

Three men in the survey job shared with their wives and a number of others had organised part time work so they could share the breadwinner and caring roles with their partners who also worked part time. Although the caring role was in most cases shared with a partner, men are also heads of one parent families either due to divorce or, in two instances, the death of a partner.

The following case history illustrates other new ways of working, such as having two jobs in two bases, including at home.

Martin Rathfelder works from home part of the time as a Welfare Rights Officer for Manchester City Council:

> " *I used to have two jobs both on a jobshare basis. One was for a very small computer company which was interesting but seemed rather precarious. A friend and I decided to apply as a job share and at the same time share one of the jobs we then had with the City Council. So we were job sharing two jobs between us. When my wife became ill I thought I could not work for a small company which required a lot of travelling.*

My boss is very tolerant, he doesn't much mind what hours I do so long as I am doing a reasonable amount of work. If the kids are ill or something has to be seen to, like the gas man coming, then I stay at home and work. Unlike most people in the City Council I don't have a clock machine. The effect of that is probably that I do more than the 35 hours work I am supposed to do. My wife died and I have two children to look after so I go home at 3:30 most days, make their tea, and then carry on working. I get help from people who pick the kids up from school for me or invite them round to tea, or take them places. I've talked to female single parents about how much help I get and I'm not sure they get quite so much.

I still effectively do two jobs for Manchester City Council. I am a Welfare Rights Officer based at a hospital. I mainly give advice to individual members of the public who have problems with their social security. My work also includes delivering training sessions to groups of people, staff of various organisations. As well as giving people advice I write letters for them, represent them at tribunals and put pressure on various officials. The other job is in computer development for the advice service which I largely do at home. In order to do that I require a bit of peace and quiet which is more easily come by at home than in the office.

The Council have a very complicated system which they call flexitime, which isn't in the least bit flexible! I don't work the core hours, because core hours are from ten till four, and in my situation not much help if you have to go and pick your children up at half past three. When I was on flexitime any work you did after half past six, for example, didn't count as work. I found that although I was working the hours, the hours that I had done weren't to be counted.

I tell people to ring me at home and even if I am doing something else, I will talk to them because computer problems need to be sorted out while they are happening. I think on the whole it is at least as easy for my colleagues to contact me as it is for me to contact them because the nature of the job is that people are often out of their office. I've had the opportunity to develop new skills, go to events, learn how to do things with a computer that I didn't do before. **"**

It is interesting to note that the flexitime scheme could not provide the flexibility that he needed.

In 1992 120,000 one parent families were headed by men according to *Population Trends*. Caring responsibilities are not restricted to childcare. One man was caring for a sick partner as well as a child and was very pleased when he saw a half time post advertised. The responsibilities of caring for elderly, sick and disabled relatives make it very difficult for workers to remain in full time, inflexible employment. The *General Household Survey* estimates there are 6.8 million people caring for someone who is sick, elderly or disabled. Of these 2.9 million are men.

Men and retirement

In the words of Professor Charles Handy retirement has become *"a technical term signifying release or a key to new possibilities"*. Opportunities for flexible working can provide an ideal solution for men and women reaching retirement age to develop their portfolio of activities. Early retirement from a full time post on a full pension gave one local authority officer the financial security to seek part time employment and develop his community and leisure interests. A former retired police officer in receipt of a good pension now works as a Minerals Monitoring Assistant and his view is that *"for people in my position part time working is entirely acceptable"*. However, many men are on low incomes and do not have access to the same opportunities.

Men who opt for phased retirement within their organisations are very enthusiastic.

A Graduate Assessor who works in the private sector two or three days per week, seven to nine hours per day during the recruitment season states that he *"saw his as a good opportunity to continue to use my knowledge, interest and expertise, to supplement income, and keep in touch with business. Apart from that it's fun"*.

However some men facing retirement are anxious. What will they do in the future, when so much of their personal identity and sense of self-worth has been given over to the organisation? *Third Age Careers* highlighted some of the fears and resentment of the prospect of inactivity along with providing solid advice about managing career transitions. Retirement is an opportunity for men to do something new and to change cultures successfully.

The Carnegie Inquiry into ageing suggested that employers are unlikely to reappraise policies towards older workers in the immediate future. A Library Attendant who worked part time did so because of *"ageism – employers will not employ over 55s"*. However, there is a demographic time bomb ticking in the background. In 1951, there were only 21 pensioners per 100 workers in the population. According to *Social Trends* this figure is set to double over the next decade. The Institute of Personnel and Development (IPD) in its statement on Age and Employment said:

"Greater use of flexible working and reduced hours will need to be considered for employees who have a preference to alter the balance of their working and personal lives. This will be an important business issue for employers seeking cost effective and efficient ways of using people's skills as the labour market mix continues to change."

The labour force is moving towards an increasing proportion of part time, casual and self employed jobs filled disproportionately by women and older men. The trend for more early retirements is set to continue as employers reduce staff by improving the financial attractiveness of their packages. An Assistant Divisional Finance Officer thinks that men and women who have worked 30-40 years full time should be given the opportunity to gradually 'wind-down' to retirement. *"Instead of wishing to work full time to age 60 and then retiring unemployed, people should be able to work, say from age 55 to 65, on a part time time basis, ie semi-retirement and gradually adjust to the 'tempo' of an older life."*

There is a sound business case for employers to match the talent, experience and skills of older workers with work which might need to be done in a more creative way. Offering flexible work options as part of a retirement package can help to enhance competitiveness on the part of the employer along with leading to enhanced quality of life on the part of the employee.

Quality of life and other interests

Men indicated in the survey that they were keen to work flexibly for other reasons. A number were involved in community activities ranging from being a Lay Preacher, to meals on wheels. Three men had taken career breaks in order to study, one for an MSc, one for an MBA and another for a PhD. Another was studying a foreign language and a GP was carrying out research.

The following case history illustrates how flexibility can contribute to the development of a career by allowing time to gain extra qualifications.

Gary Richardson worked as a Corporate Officer for NatWest looking after a portfolio of corporate clients. He is currently making use of the Bank's Employment Break Scheme to study full time for an MBA at Cranfield:

> " I had joined NatWest as a graduate four years ago. I initially knew about the scheme as a woman who was on it used to come in every year to do two weeks' work. My initial impression was that it was for people who wanted time off to look after new born babies or sick parents. However, when I had decided to resign to do an MBA, I was talking to my administration manager about my resignation and he suggested I apply for the Employment Break Scheme. He phoned up the Personnel Manager at Regional Office who said he'd be happy to consider my application. I applied and it was granted. There were no problems.
>
> I'm taking a year's break which started in October 1994. As my first degree was in Business Administration, taking an MBA had been on my mind for a while. With all the bank cut backs I thought now would be the time to go for it. I'm 28 and I've got no commitments so far, so I just thought it was best to do it full time in one year as opposed to the part time course which takes two years. I am financed at Cranfield via a special bank loan for MBA students.
>
> My colleagues were pleased about what I was doing and my boss was keen. He had the attitude that he'd got on in life and appreciated that other people wanted to as well. I was quite surprised and pleased that NatWest gave me the chance to do this.
>
> There are huge culture changes taking place within NatWest. However, it is still mainly women who are taking advantage of flexible working. I didn't think of it until someone suggested it to me. I have written a piece for the Bank's Employment Break Newsletter. "

Leisure interests such as mountaineering and gardening were mentioned by others. This man wanted to further develop his freelance artwork, which has been very successful.

Dennis Foster now works as a Norwich Community Alarm Service Operator on a basic 25.5 hours a week for Norwich City Council.

    ❝ *I am one of a team of seven operators running an emergency computer controlled console linked to users via the BT network. This provides cover for about 7,000 elderly or disabled people, who live alone and may need support. They have alarm units they can press which act like a two way radio. It's a 24 hour, 365 day a year service. We're classified as part time and work a rolling shift system, with morning, afternoon and night shifts each week. I work a 25.5 hour week with a standby shift available to cover sickness, holidays or absence. Our supervisor works a 9-5, five day week, and is on call in an emergency.*

This working arrangement suits me very well as I'm also an artist and sculptor. When I was made redundant in 1983, I studied art for two years as a mature student. I've been involved in art all my life.

In 1990 whilst working as a travelling salesman, I saw this job advertised and thought it could give me an opportunity to do more art work because I'd only done about two paintings that year, and a little sculpture work on a commission I had received. Last year I saw the placement of this work, the design and making of a bronze sculpture based on a ballet dedicated to the memory of choreographer, Sir Kenneth Macmillan. It is now situated in the grounds of a stately home which is open to the public. I wouldn't be interested in work which prevented me pursuing my creative activities.

I'm aware the three men on our team may be seen as oddities, due to the hours worked. Many we speak to over the air waves assume we are women, also voluntary and not employed. They find it hard to accept that we have chosen this career. The general view is that men choose full time work and that women accept part time more readily. The fact that on some days I become house husband and do the cleaning, laundry, shopping and cooking seems odd to some people – but not to me.

Provided the structure of my work does not radically alter due to competitive tendering, I'll be here until retirement. Previously, I used to work 13 hour days, six days a week professionally with the elderly, for the princely sum of £7,000 a year. One day, stuck in a traffic jam I thought, 'Do I really want to be doing this for 20 years, until I'm 65?' Now, a full time job would have to pay a lot for me to consider changing my lifestyle. Work is not the be-all and end-all in life, fulfilment is more important. Unfortunately in our society work is the thing we are judged by. It's not who you are, but what you do that counts. In developing and fulfilling ourselves maybe this will change.

The desire for an improved quality of life was mentioned by a number of men: *"You could create a culture where people accept only working four days and that is a lot healthier. I think four days is plenty really. Then there's this awful two day weekend where everyone has to be happy and get on beautifully together because they are back into the system again on Monday morning. And then if you don't get on well and have a nice time you get terribly stressed out and get angry. If you could loosen it all up a bit there would be more time and space in which to enjoy yourself, see family and friends, travel, join clubs or grow vegetables."*
Voluntary Sector Worker

Political interests and public service featured on some agendas as in the following case study.

Peter Scott is a Senior Lecturer teaching computer programming in the School of Computing and Management Sciences, Sheffield Hallam University.

I've been job sharing for seven years, I work three days a week and my partner does two. With lecturing it's relatively easy to arrange a job share. I have three-fifths of 40 hours a week class contact time. To begin with we also shared an administration job between us as the admissions tutor for one of our courses.

There were three reasons why I wanted to work flexibly. First I'd been quite active in the Green Party and I wanted to spend more time doing that. By the time you'd done your five days a week work there was very little time and energy left for other things I really wanted to do. Secondly, I'm doing up an old house and I wanted to make faster progress with it and I like gardening and wanted more time off work to do these things. Thirdly, my kids have been going through orthodontic treatment and it's nice to be able to take them without having to rush around, taking time off work. It's been really good for me to have time to spend with them, they are 16 and 14.

What I initially asked to do was not very ambitious, I simply asked to have one day a week off and work four days, but this was vetoed by my boss. About a year passed and my wife and I decided I would take a job share, because I knew a colleague at work wanted to do one, so I spoke to her while she was on maternity leave and said I'd do it. It was quite funny because she'd only asked the women in the department if they wanted to do it! It worked out really well because she didn't really want 50:50, she wanted less, so she was happy to have two days and I was happy to have three. It was quite nice that the pair of us between us had actually created a job. The political parties talk about creating jobs, but we actually did it and somebody in my department has a job which they may not have had otherwise. The University has a job share policy and there were no problems in getting the job share approved.

When you're in a job share you tend to work more solidly and you can miss out on informal gossip. When we shared the admin job we both used to work on Wednesday afternoon, but we also phoned each other up as well. I now work Monday, Wednesday, Thursday during this term because the classes I've got happen to fall on these days, but it varies between semesters.

One of my reasons for doing the job share was that work was taking up too much energy and I've noticed that this last year or so, I've been very keen on work. I'm much more interested in it than when I was doing it five days a week and sometimes I find it a bit of a nuisance that I'm not doing it full time. But I know very well that if I was doing it five days a week I would feel it was too much. It's all to do with balance. When I started the job share I thought I was totally off balance, I thought I was spending far too much time and energy at work and not enough doing other things in life. I have a lot more variety in life than I would if I was working five days a week and then rushing around trying to spend the rest of my life in the remaining two days and my family see more of me. Some days I'm in before the kids come home, some days they're in first. My wife works full time as a Deputy Head.

I'm still the only man I know about in the organisation who doesn't work full time. There are men on temporary contracts, but in most cases they would like a full time permanent contract, but with increasing casualisation in education they can't get it, so they have to take what they can get. A lot of students just assume that I'm just out making money in the other two days, particularly because I work in computing. They think I'm doing consultancy work. If they knew that sometimes I spend a day cooking for the freezer or a day in the garden!

All lecturers work very long hours. I think that people are very wrapped up in their work in many cases. The difference now is that they feel under pressure to be like that and I see it rubbing off on the administrative staff. I was in on a Saturday morning recently to pick something up and found a surprising number of administration staff in.

I think that some people do view what I do as slightly odd, but I stood as a Green Party candidate in the European Elections, so they know that I've got very different attitudes to most people.

One of the reasons I wanted to work part time is that there are four million unemployed. I just think it's terribly wrong that some people have got more work than they can handle and more income than they need, and other people are totally denied it. My wife had about seven years off work when we had kids and then she went back to work. I thought with all the unemployment that it wasn't really fair that the pair of us should have two full time jobs between us.

I was a very conventional person and when I first came across another man working part time, about 16 years ago, I though it was very strange, but when I came to know him it made sense. I realise now that his ideas were very Green. He lived then the way I try to do now.

I don't see myself going back to full time, although I've got the opportu5 nity, because the other half of my job share is resigning and management asked me if I wanted to do the whole job again, but I'm not going to.

Another man gave his reason as *"a personal desire to live in Scotland – the flexible work arrangements followed this"*.

Men and other paid work

"My job sharing and career break are accepted by my colleagues. However, when I was doing a 'double job share' in 1992 I think that there was some ill feeling amongst my colleagues from my 'original' post and I felt that I was torn between the two jobs – almost being fought over by two different sections."
Training Coordinator

Three men said that their prime reason for working flexibly in their main job was so that they could carry out other paid work, this included one GP who job shared and also worked as a Police Surgeon. Three men in the survey were doing two jobs on a part time basis. One man combined three jobs.

Peter Carr, aged 47, is based in East Anglia and does three part time jobs: firefighter, caretaker of the local village hall and casual coach driving. To him this working style is a strength. *"Being relatively skilled, I feel that employers actually treat me better because I don't work for them full time. They and I, don't feel that my whole future is bound up with them. It might be different if I was a shop assistant or cleaner."*

Chapter three:
The flexible patterns men work

Men and flexitime

"In the scheme I work there is the ability to build up hours to take leave or time off if problems occur with the children. This scheme means that I do not need to use my annual leave entitlement to cover care for the children."
Architectural Technician, local authority

Men were very enthusiastic about flexitime as it is a practical way to create space to enable them to meet some domestic responsibilities and occasionally just to create some spare time for themselves. Flexible Working Hours (FWH) or flexitime schemes allow employees to choose, within set limits, the times they start and finish work. They also permit an employee to carry over any excess or deficit in hours beyond an accounting period (usually a month), with the option of taking 'flexi-leave'. Flexitime remains a popular option and remains firmly fixed in most local authority terms and conditions. A Cycling Officer for a local authority states, *"I fully use flexitime to suit my own needs, ie taking partner to station, daughter to childminder etc"*.

Some flexitime also has a downside. A Volunteer Coordinator for a local authority says that *"it does allow me to alter my hours somewhat, but flexitime often means that I end up working unsocial hours to get the job done."* However, *"shifts can be swapped if necessary"*, claims a Community Alarm System Operator. Flexitime claims a Neighbourhood Coordinator *"allows an early 8am start which I use to clear work and plan work for the day as well as meaning I can travel on more stress free roads prior to rush hour traffic"*.

But there can be rigidity even within a flexitime scheme. A Training Coordinator questions the core time of his authority's scheme:

"Flexible working hours can be worked between 8am-10am, 12-2pm and 4-7pm each day, with 10-12 and 2-4 as 'core time'. I would find it more convenient if I was allowed to begin at 7am and I believe that the employer's refusal to grant a general extension of flexitime to the 7-8 period is unreasonable, given that the building is physically open and there is a security guard on duty this time. Given that schemes such as term time working and annualised hours are given consideration, this inflexibility in the flexitime arrangements is puzzling."

The following father has worked out his own system of flexitime.

David Rice is a Planning Analyst at BP Exploration, one of the three core businesses of BP (the other two being BP Oil and BP Chemicals). BP Exploration represents about 55 per cent of the capital employed in BP, one of the world's largest petroleum companies. Unusually for a senior executive he leaves work at 4:30pm most days to collect his children, aged three and eight.

> " *I have two children aged three and eight. I think I was very influenced when we were living and working in Norway where our first child was born. I think the whole culture of Norwegian society is very different to this culture. It's very child orientated, official working hours in Norway are 8 to 3:30 in the afternoon, so I could work till 5 and do a long day and still be home by 5:10, because there's no commuting. So that affected my feelings a lot about how things could be.*

I have a partner, who has a full time job and is a doctor. This took away my fear of redundancy because there is some financial security with a working partner. I don't know if I would have held such strong views if I had a partner who was at home all day, so that I could be late home and I could go away more. We have a day nanny, at home, and she comes at half seven in the morning, and leaves at five fifteen, so one of us has to be back by then every day. I leave at 4:30.

People generally come in earlier than they used to and work hard, work late and do work at home, so it's very hard to know what flexible means. In that context, it's not 9-5 flexitime. But I leave work at 4:30 most days to collect our children. I regard that as flexible working because most people don't leave here until 6 o'clock, some nights 10 or 11 o'clock, if there's a project they are very busy with. I start about 8 and I'm not the first one in. There's probably two people in when I get in, in the morning, who've been in since about 7:30 and I'm certainly the first person to leave at 4:30.

It all comes down to the immediate line manager. It's not the corporate philosophy that's important. The chairman, the chief executives and managing directors can say what they believe to be the case and they can try and lay down cultures for BP but it comes down to the individual line manager and what that person believes. I have worked with line managers, one in particular who used to come in at 4 o'clock, and say, 'isn't it about time you were going.' He used to actually walk down the corridor and remind me to go home. Other managers will spit blood and threaten you with all sorts of things, when you say, 'I'm sorry I must go now because I'm collecting the children.' I think it is about men's perceptions of women. What I tell managers is to think of me as a single mother and if that's too difficult to think of me as a single father, to pretend I'm bringing up children on my own, and then react. I tell them not to assume I've got a woman at home who is looking after my children and that they should imagine I don't have anyone else and then tell me not to go home – it does change people's reactions. I think if men can change their perception of men then it actually changes their perception of women, as well.

Many men are now living in situations where they work away from home, either part of the week or all of the week, and travel back at weekends to their families. So we now have men who don't see their families during the week – it's a form of migrant labour. I work with people who spend three nights a week down here and four up there. That's their job. They'll travel down Sunday night, stay two or three nights down here, then travel back to Scotland, where their home is. I think people are very frightened of losing their jobs. My argument is that you can deliver what's needed in demanding jobs without having to do those things.

John Harvey-Jones (who was the Chairman of ICI) used to leave work at 5:15 and go home. I work flexitime in a way and leaving work that early does mean arranging meetings carefully. People start meetings at 5 or 6 o'clock, so I can't go to some of those. But I use IT a lot so I will sometimes go home, and at 7 or 8 o'clock in the evening I will put my computer on to see if I have got any mail. If I've got a fairly solid piece of work I'll stay at home for a day, and work. Now when that's working well, it's not a problem, because as long as you deliver the products, the output, it doesn't matter how you do it. But it does create a lot of strain at times, because people want to talk, and they want you to visit and be there sometimes.

Some men commented in the interviews that because their employers did not yet offer paternity leave schemes, flexitime became an invaluable tool when combined with extended holidays to cover the birth of a child. However, flexitime is not so widespread in the private sector and one employer, *Clerical and Medical Insurance* has recently abandoned its system of flexitime. They say that their new culture of paying people to do a job, rather than to sit at a desk for a fixed number of hours, clashed with the notion of counting hours and minutes.

Men and term time working

"I'd like to carry on with this arrangement until the children are at school, and then it might be more appropriate to work more in line with the school terms. So I would still foresee flexible working, but I think it will be different as we go through life."
Manager, private sector

Term time working gives fathers a real chance to get to know their children. It means that a father can spend relaxed periods of time with his children during holidays instead of the usual few hours at the end of a tiring day. Employees remain on a permanent contract as either full or part time employees, but they then have the right to (unpaid) leave of absence during the school holidays. Unpaid leave during schools holidays is usually an extra eight or nine weeks, in addition to the paid annual leave entitlement of say five weeks. Holidays are not usually taken during term time, although some schemes specify that four weeks of annual leave need only be taken during the school holidays. This allows a few days to be reserved for emergencies.

The timing of the unpaid absence and the bulk of paid leave would have to be determined at the beginning of the year to allow management to sort out staffing schedules. One man identified term time working as an invaluable option as it overcomes the problem of childcare in the holidays. The following case history sets out the practicalities and management of such a scheme. It also describes the process of negotiation needed with colleagues who may feel under pressure to take on additional work during the period of absence.

Shaheer Mohammed works on a term time basis as a Voluntary Organisations Liaison Officer for Leicester City Council.

" *My post was advertised for 18.5 hours a week. I was grateful for that because I was also a carer for my wife and daughter and was looking for something which would permit me flexibility in hours at work. I had been looking after my wife for about two years before I applied for the job. I was made redundant in my last job and was living in London at the time. Then we moved to Leicester because she wanted to be close to her birthplace for her last few days. We moved even though I didn't have a job. I used to do things like consultancy work. That suited me to a certain degree but obviously it wasn't regular money. After she died I had a full time childminder. My daughter at the time was five and was in school. I just needed someone to get her home from school for a few hours and I thought it would only be until 6:00pm so I could get home.*

Obviously it's not an easy thing with a recent bereavement and looking after a child. I found I was getting quite exhausted and because of that I was taking more time off. After some-

thing like that you can't really keep working full time without it having some sort of an effect on your system. I was taking more time off which I am sure was looked upon sympatheti- cally because of my circumstances. Then during one of the sickness consultations we came across the term time working scheme that Leicester City Council runs and we didn't think of that before. I thought it was a great idea. I worked out the hours and the money it would cost me to employ a childminder during the holidays and as a matter of fact I think I was better off in the long run. I was less stressed and I could spend more time with my little girl. I do feel that some firms I have worked for would be totally unsympathetic towards people with the same circumstances as myself.

I have the whole of the summer holidays off and all yearly holidays off. My contract stipu- lates, I can't quite remember exactly, about 35 weeks. I have a new contract. I get paid the same amount each month and it's averaged out over the year. I work 37 hours a week. We also have a flexi arrangement. It means that if I have evening meetings or work any extra hours instead of taking that as overtime I save it off as time off in lieu or flexi, then when it's my daughter's Christmas play or she needs to go somewhere I can book off time that's not term time work.

When I was negotiating this arrangement we decided it was going to be fairly quiet any- way because during the eight week holidays there is always someone out anyway. It depends very much on the type of work, what sort of demands there are, how many peo- ple can cover my post while I'm away. Thinking about it now most jobs would allow some sort of flexibility because people are away. While I'm on term time working I do feel that I would have less chances of getting a job with more responsibilities if I wanted one. Also fur- ther training might be difficult, because you feel you are not at work enough anyway.

I read about Leicester's scheme to help carers come back to work in the papers they sent out. This was one of the things that attracted me to the job. As I had been out of work for two years that was another thing I took advantage of and it paid off. I think it all depends on the manager and whether he or she knows what is on offer. Perhaps the communica- tion is not good. I have spoken with other single parents in the Council since and they were not aware that term time working exists. They could publicise it and say that in exception- al circumstances you can negotiate term time working or reduced hours.

Knowing my circumstances family and friends are very supportive. I feel that I have an eas- ier time as a single father than a single mother. I think generally it's not a common thing to be a single parent father. I certainly get a lot of moral support. I find people are more sympathetic on the evenings when I have to attend management committee meetings, especially as I have to make arrangements so short notice is difficult. They are fairly open and sensitive about it. Whether they would be with a woman, I don't know, I shouldn't

99

think so. If she were a Project Officer and single parent I'm not sure she would have the same treatment in that respect. I think work colleagues are more sympathetic. I think you are treated very differently in a nice way.

Formal term time only policies outside education remain an unusual employment practice, although some government departments do grant short term 'special leave' to enable parents to look after children in the school holidays. New guidance for civil servants has put this on a formal basis, known as 'part year' appointments.

Men working reduced hours

Part time

"The main issue is the status of part time working – that is how it is perceived. In areas traditionally dominated by women (secretarial, libraries etc) it is seen as a good means of maintaining a flexible workforce on a long term basis. This is not a commonly held belief in male dominated areas of work!"
Volunteer Coordinator, local authority

The most popular option among men was reducing hours. It seems an obvious solution to combining work, family and other interests. Over 67 per cent of men in the survey worked part time. This included 27 per cent who worked on a job share basis with the majority employed by local authorities.

The number of employees working part time (less than 30 hours in Britain) continued to grow throughout the 1980s to around a quarter of the workforce – a total of 5.4 million by summer 1994. Currently, 14 per cent of all part time workers are men. Around 45 per cent of all women employees work part time, compared with 7 per cent of men.

Until recently, under employment legislation, those who worked for fewer than 16 hours a week were treated less favourably than full time workers, unless they had been working for more than eight hours for five years or more for the same employer. However as from February 1995 new regulations repeal the requirement to work a minimum number of hours per week in order for the week to count as a period of continuous service.

The following man has opted to reduce his hours to devote more time to his children and other interests. Reduced hours do not seem to be an impediment to increased outputs or energy, judging by the range of things he is involved in!

Tony Cornah is a Senior Systems Programmer, in the Department of Automatic Control and Systems Engineering at Sheffield University. He has worked part time for 16 years in two different jobs and is currently on a half time contract.

❝ *I'm responsible for making sure a network of work stations for researchers and students runs smoothly, for installing new software and for recommending computing strategy to the Department's Policy Committee. I also organise the work of the other programmers in the Department. There are two parts to the network and because I work part time the administration of the other half of the network is delegated to one of the other programmers. At the moment on top of that half time job, I'm working one day a week doing pure programming for a particular research team until September. I'm also doing another day a week until June preparing a distance learning module for the programme the Department runs in Singapore.*

The main reason I wanted to reduce my hours was because I wanted to be involved in bringing up the children my partner, Polly, and I were planning to have. At this stage we both started to look for part time jobs. At the time I was working in the University Computing Services, and they were reluctant to have me working part time there, but I found out that the programmer at a Research Unit attached to the University was about to leave and I was employed half time and they got a new graduate full time. I was still working full time when Polly became pregnant but I had the part time job organised by then.

The attitude was very different when I took up my present post ten years ago. I heard of my current job when the current programmer was pregnant and wanted to come back part time after having her child. I was offered the other half of the job (through an internal appointment) and that was fairly straightforward, there were no problems of attitude.

At the moment I've overloaded myself again and I'm really noticing how much more stressed I feel. When I come home I know that I've got three things I need to be doing at that time, so there's not the same opportunity for relaxation. So working fewer hours has had a very beneficial effect and I hope it will again. I've had a lot more time to pursue other things, particularly in the early years with the children. I've been to assemblies at the children's schools. I've been able to go to the last couple of parent's evenings, whereas Polly hasn't for work reasons. I've had an opportunity to play more sport than I would have otherwise, to do more decorating and other practical work in the house and generally just more time, reading, walking and other interests.

My father's in hospital at the moment and when he comes out I will be able to visit him from Thursday evening to Monday evening if this is necessary without interrupting my work. *This will make a lot of difference to me, so that's important.*

The ability to work flexibly when you've got young children is vital, as well as when they start school. I think that extra flexibility enables your relationships with your children to develop more than they would otherwise. I have changed my pattern of work several times. I used to work half a day each day, when the children were younger and when Polly was working a lot less than now. Now they are older I work two short full days and one long half day and that fits in with being at home when they come home from school or meeting them from school when they were younger.

I don't particularly think I want to work full time. When I'm older, even if I haven't got the sport I'm sure that there will be other things I'll want to do. It's not that I don't enjoy the work, it's just that I enjoy other things as well.

It seems to me that it would be far better if the existing work could be more equitably distributed, because it seems as though, despite the fact that there are so many people unemployed, that the people who do have jobs tend to work under pressure and overtime. It would be far better if more people were employed. I know there are skills shortages in particular areas, but more people working fewer hours is a better way of going about things It would be good to have something like the Scandinavian model for parental leave where the parents decide how to arrange caring between them for the early years of their children's lives.

Job sharing

"The job share is with my wife. We are free to arrange the hours of work between us."
Consultant in the NHS

Men are now discovering that one of the easiest ways of transforming a full time job into a part time job is to share it. It opens up the world of part time work. Job sharing is a way of working where two people voluntarily share the responsibilities of one full time job, dividing the pay, holidays and other benefits between them according to the number of hours worked. It is becoming a more accepted way of introducing 'part time' hours into jobs which have traditionally only been available on a full time basis, particularly at senior and managerial levels. The number of such arrangements in more senior, professional and technical posts is increasing. Manual workers are still underrepresented, perhaps because of lower salary levels even though many local authority schemes are open to both manual and non-manual workers.

In the early 1980s employees mainly negotiated a job share on an individual basis. Local authorities pioneered the development of full job share schemes offering the option widely among employees. A recent survey of flexible working in Local

Government carried out by New Ways to Work found that 62 per cent of the 249 authorities surveyed now have a formal job share scheme. A number of Civil Service departments also developed job sharing policies during this period. A survey of 320 companies carried out by *Personnel Today* in 1994 found that 26 per cent used job sharing.

Just over a quarter (28) of the 106 men in our survey were job sharing and three were sharing with their wives, including the following solicitor.

Tim Powell has shared the post of Assistant Solicitor for a Solicitors firm in South London for five years with his wife, Deirdre.

" I do civil litigation covering all areas but mostly personal injury, housing, and a mix of contract and negligence claims. There are five solicitors, one legal executive and then a secretary for each of them and other support staff, 16 altogether. I work three days a week, Mondays, Wednesdays and Thursdays. My wife Deirdre works Tuesdays and Fridays. We jointly manage and supervise our secretary. She works full time and provides the continuity.

We took the decision at the time our daughter was born. She was born November 1989 and I was working full time for a firm of solicitors in the West End. I wanted to leave that firm and when Katie was born, I left the job and took six weeks 'paternity leave'. It was at that time when we discussed bringing up Katie, that we hit upon the idea of doing a job share. We decided to do that so that we could bring up the children ourselves rather than have a childminder.

Once we had decided to do a job share we had to find someone who would buy the idea. Deirdre met a mutual acquaintance who is a partner in a firm of Solicitors in Tulse Hill, South London, and she suggested that we could come and work for him as a jobshare. His immediate response was that it would not work, but after thought explored it further. We were invited to put in a joint application, and we were called for interview to explain ourselves, and try to persuade. Because it was novel there was resistance to it. They did not know how it would work in practice. How would we make the arrangements, divide up our work, how would we tell the outside world, what would the reaction be, what would our clients say to it, how would we cope with emergencies, how would there be continuity of the work? The firm was hesitant, rightly so, with a new idea that they had no experience of. But in the end they were effectively getting two for the price of one, (the only extra cost was getting two practising certificates instead of one). It is a marginal increase in costs. There is not a long hours culture at my firm. I think they are very positive because they have seen how it works and they are very used to it.

Working three days a week is wonderful. I spend more days at home than I do at work. The job is still stressful and there are times when you still have to meet deadlines – and so you have to be more organised to meet the deadline while you are at work. I can't leave the work till the Friday because I won't be there. We don't share clients. When I worked full time you could often leave things till the next day.

I am very fortunate that I am bringing up the children, so I have had contact with them from their earliest stages. When Katie was 18 months, two years, I used to take her off to a mini-gym every Tuesday. That was just a wonderful thing to do – helping my daughter bounce on a trampoline. Or walking around the park pushing my son on the swings. It sounds idyllic and it still is. If I was working five days a week I would only see them at weekends. Now Katie is at school in the reception class, I go to the school on a Friday morning and help out in the class. I read to the children. That is something I would never have had the chance to do if I was working five days a week.

There is the downside to everything – that we are operating on one salary. If we both worked full time and employed someone to look after the children we would be miles better off, there is no doubt about that. We could have foreign holidays, and two cars and a bigger house. We could be richer but we have chosen not to be. That is the trade off. But compared to other people we have a good salary so we can't complain.

I suppose being husband and wife we talk a lot about the job at home which might be seen as a disadvantage. I tend to switch off after nine o'clock anyway, but Deirdre likes to continue talking about these things after nine o'clock, but we've always talked about work even before the job share. It's very difficult to say what other disadvantage there is, just the money. Even that's not such a great disadvantage.

Some of our clients might wish that we were there five days a week so they could have us at the end of a telephone whenever they wanted. But we've had so few comments about it in five years the problem hasn't arisen. Very often solicitors are out of the office anyway doing things in court sometimes for days on end, so the expectation that we should be at the end of a phone five days a week is quite unrealistic. In any case as long as you've got

someone who can take messages and pass them on and if there is an emergency then who-
ever's at work will deal with it anyway so there's always someone to cover.
I can see that might be a problem, but we have very little experience of
clients being dissatisfied.

Four day week

"It is rare to see four day week jobs advertised. Fortunately I am fairly happy in my pre-sent job. I earn enough for our family's needs on four days a week. I spend roughly one day a week doing voluntary work for a cycle campaign pressure group, and approximately one day in our large garden. We also have two young children."
Computing Officer, university

There were a number of men in the survey who were working a four day week and for them this was the best reduced hours option. It gave a balance between meeting financial needs, particularly where they had children and allowing them more time for family and other needs.

However, a number specifically mentioned that they had asked for a four day week and that was not an option.

"I had no difficulty in going job share or in taking a career break. However, there was once a time when I wanted to work a 4 day week (and only be paid for 4 days, of course) and the answer I got was a definite no! Sometimes people do want a halfway house between job sharing (1/2 week) and full time (whole week) working, but the facility to do this doesn't seem to exist for me."
Training Coordinator, local authority

Voluntary reduced hours

"Budget cuts mean the organisation is looking for ways to save money. Voluntary reduced hours has become one way."
Head of Administration & Finance, local authority

One way of creating a half way house between full time and half time is a Voluntary Reduced Work Time (V-time) scheme. These allow employees to voluntarily trade income for time off. In principle people are given the option of reducing their full time working hours, usually by between five and 50 per cent, for a specified period, usually a year, with the right to return to full time at the end of that period. The time can be taken by reducing the working day, or week or by taking a block of time off in the year.

V-time schemes have been in operation in the USA since 1976. The first experiment was introduced in Santa Clara County, California and was negotiated by the public services union; a survey of union members had found that there was more interest in shorter hours than in higher pay. Since then the option has been introduced in a number of local authorities in the USA.

Although formal schemes have not developed in the same way in the UK, there are a number of individual cases, where employees have negotiated a personal arrangement in this way. As part of a scheme *Flexible ways of working for carers and employees with disabilities*, Sheffield City Council have introduced a V-time Option, on an individually negotiated basis.

Four per cent of men indicated in the survey that they were working on a voluntary reduced hours basis.

Men working from home

"My arrangement works because I work quite independently. I arrange my own workload. My department encourages flexible ways of working – working from home, use of portable computers, mobile phones, pagers, phone chargecards."
Principal Trading Standards Officer, local authority

Teleworking, telecommuting, remote or homeworking are considered as arrangements where salaried employees spend all or some of their working week at home or working from home. They have the status of 'employee' within their organisation and a contract of employment. They may be either working from home as a base, working from home (either with or without on-line computer links) or partly in an office and partly at home. The trend towards teleworking is worldwide.

Many teleworking schemes have been set up on an ad hoc basis, with individuals or groups of employees working out their own arrangements with their employers. Two men in the survey were working from home as a base, but seven were working from home for part of the time. This varied from those who worked a certain number of days a week from home to a planning analyst, in the private sector who says, *"I spend a day home occasionally – about once every three or four weeks. I have a home computer and phone link to office and fax machine. I use my home office evenings/ weekends to make up time"*.

The following case history provides a role model from a distance.

Kevin Attfield works at NatWest as Manager, Strategic Planning and is based three days a week in London and teleworks two days a week from his home in

Scotland. He has four children who are 12, 10, 8 and 4.

> **"** *We moved to Scotland because my wife and I just didn't feel at home in the South East. We explored several options including living abroad. We'd booked a fortnight's holiday in Scotland (with no ulterior motive!) and then at the end of the first week, quite independently, both realised this was where we wanted to live. This wasn't the 'wouldn't it be nice to live here?' type of thought you sometimes get on holiday. This was different. There were so many factors to do with the place, the people, and so on. But there was something even deeper than that. We knew that was the place. But it was absurd! Four hundred miles away from where I worked, and our families in the South. So there were obviously going to be some practical difficulties. It took about just over two years to make it a viable proposition. Partly because of the different legal systems, conveyancing and so forth, it nearly didn't happen.*

I've worked at NatWest for 14 or 15 years – ever since I graduated. I'm slightly ashamed to say that I didn't raise the move with the Bank until after it had happened, because the whole thing was so on/off. I had to do three things: find a buyer for my house, negotiate for the new house, and find a new job. To get all three things to coincide was almost impossible, so we settled for two out of three and at the last minute it did all go through. The move took place and I took a few days off. When I got back my boss asked whether I'd done anything exciting. Moved house. Far? Scotland. It took quite some time before he realised I wasn't winding him up. We went out to lunch and talked through all the reasons behind it. Obviously one of the questions was about my intentions towards the Bank. I was quite open about it and said I think I would probably have to leave at some stage – I didn't think carrying on in London would be a sustainable proposition and had more or less resigned myself to leaving. The real killer was having so little time with my family. I explained this to my boss. Slightly tongue in cheek, I suggested that if our Strategic Planning Manager got his act together, we would have some sort of policy on teleworking and I could work from home. He reacted very positively to that and said that if I put together a proposal he would look at it seriously.

There happened to be an article on teleworking around that time which mentioned a colleague in another part of the Group. I made contact and obtained a great deal of useful information about the Bank's stance on flexible working practices – the principle was endorsed at a very senior level in the Bank. I was also referred to New Ways to Work publications.

I put in a proposal. My boss came back with a request for more information on the financial side but generally supported the idea of a number of small steps rather than one great leap into the unknown. Obviously he was apprehensive about how this was going to affect other people in the office, including himself. I think we were both very cautious. So we went for a phased implementation. Either side could opt to delay the next phase and if necessary we could backtrack. We decided to keep it very simple to begin with. We didn't go and spend large amounts of money. It was a question of begging, stealing and borrowing. I already had a portable computer and tracked down an unused fax. We didn't go for video conferencing or even additional telephone lines.

We started off with two days a week teleworking initially and that is how it has stayed. The original proposal envisaged moving on to three, but two is really the right number for the job. My assistant had just joined the unit and was unsure how he would like working for someone who 'wasn't there' a lot of the time. In fact it worked out quite well. The unit is quite small (10 positions). We all have our own jobs to do, but work as a team, and he acted as intermediary. Teleworking hasn't been too much of an obstacle because I can speak to people on the phone, fax papers backwards and forwards and stay in touch with what's going on. The rest of the week I can see people face to face. On Wednesday mornings when I get in I have an update meeting with my boss and go through the work and any issues. That's followed by a team meeting. So I don't feel as though I'm not part of the unit, and nor do they.

Outside the unit there have been mixed reactions: encouragement, scepticism, interest – sometimes astonishment! Because it's a slightly unusual arrangement, and obviously tailored to local needs, it's not seen as threatening and most people haven't found it too much of a problem. Occasionally people ring up and apologise for disturbing me at home, as though I'm on leave. I'm not. I'm just working in a different place.

I try and arrange my schedule carefully but, with senior people, obviously I have to fit in with their diaries. I have to be flexible and there are times when I have to be here on Monday or Tuesday and move the days around. As an objective, though, I think it's better to keep it regular, to keep to the same days.

We don't review the teleworking arrangement formally but invariably it crops up from time to time, how things are going, any problems etc. But we don't feel we need to be religious about it.

The arrangement is more sustainable than I originally thought. I'd expected it to grind me down physically but I've adjusted to the travel and my family have adjusted to the routine. While I have my bosses' support, there is no reason for the teleworking to cease. If I found myself moved to another position, where local needs were different, then that might raise some issues.

To summarise I suppose I would say you don't need complicated technology. You need a willingness to try, trust on both sides, flexibility, and the ability to learn from mistakes and make adjustments. I think it's important to keep it simple, to build up trust and to move on as both sides feel comfortable with the arrangements.

Men taking breaks from employment

Employment/career breaks

An employment or career break is an extended period of unpaid leave from work. The intention is that at some future date the employee will return to work with the same employer at either the same level or to the same job, retaining all or most of the service related benefits. They are sometimes called retainer or re-entry schemes. During the break employer and employee keep in touch by a variety of means.

The term employment break, which is the description preferred by the Institute of Personnel and Development embraces maternity, paternity, parental and sabbatical leave. The new term, employment break, also avoids the connotations with professional jobs and high fliers that may be associated with the words career break.

Eighteen men said that they had taken an employment break and of these, nine worked in the public sector and five in the private sector, while three worked for other organisations such as the voluntary sector or for a church. Three men had taken a break to study and one of them, Gary Richardson, is featured as a case study in Chapter two.

Men think that their access to career breaks is limited in practice even if the organisation's policy includes them. For them the issues are about progressing in a career along with enjoying the benefits of a break. A Training Coordinator in a local authority thinks that management has another agenda:

"The line management doesn't have major difficulties in coping with people working job share. However, 'they' (the powers that be) have decided not to fill my post while I'm on my career break. This really made me feel as if my job just wasn't worth doing. I think this decision reflects higher thinking towards career breaks – they're probably seen as (a) a nuisance or (b) a chance to change work loads and (dare I say it?) a way of getting people to leave, more easily than might otherwise have been the case. So although the career break scheme might be intended to look like a benefit to employees, senior management may have realised its potential use as a back-door route to redeployment."

More and more companies are introducing career breaks, but they need to be thought through carefully. Rosalyn Merfield, who was involved in setting up Unilever's career break scheme, was interviewed for *New Statesman & Society*. She said that *"although there are sound business reasons for the scheme we were not particularly interested in encouraging men to do it. It would be different if retaining men were as serious a problem as retaining women, but men don't experience the same incompatibilities because it's still women who usually take most responsibility at home."*

It is recognised by Unilever that women will be the main users of the career break scheme but it is open to all managers (see case history below). Merfield also claimed that career breaks may be equal opportunities red herrings because children are still there when the career break ends and women need long term flexibility to help them balance careers and work.

Unilever is responding to this now by exploring different forms of flexible working. However very rapid increases in the number of women managers will only occur if men take more child care responsibilities and/or the assumption that business needs a core of full time, totally flexible and dedicated managers is challenged.

Julian Duxfield is an Employee Development Manager for Unilever, which is a holding company for 23 other companies in the UK. In January 1993 he began a two year long break from employment, making use of the company's Career Break Scheme.

❝ *Before my Career Break I was working as an Operating Personnel Manager in one of the Unilever companies, Lever Industrial, which employs about 800 people, on two sites. I'd been working for Unilever for four years, but in two different companies. My partner and I had no children at the time and we had always wanted to take some time out of full time employment. Eighteen months prior to the break we talked about it and came to the conclusion that if we didn't do it now we'd never do it. We both decided to take some time off our jobs and in the end we both took career breaks.*

I went to my boss explaining what I wanted to do. At the time I wasn't quite sure of the details of the Career Break Scheme. In my role as Personnel Manager, I hadn't ever put anyone on a career break. However, the existence of a scheme made it easier for me. The scheme is predominantly used by women going off to have children. There is a maximum of five years, minimum one year and we try and get people to do work on a consultancy basis for four weeks a year while they are away. It doesn't always happen, but it's good to keep people in touch. I didn't do any work, but I kept in touch with my ex boss. That's the

key thing – that you do keep in touch with what's happening.

My boss was quite supportive of me taking a career break because I would have moved out of that job quite shortly anyway, as I was ready for another career move. I talked to him five months before I left. The person who was running the Career Break Scheme within Unilever at the time was very supportive and she was quite pleased to have a male on it.

My Career Break started in January 1993. I had three reasons for taking the break. First we spent six months travelling around through China, Pakistan and SE Asia. Secondly I wanted to do an MSc in Industrial Relations and Personnel Management at the London School of Economics. The third reason was that I also do a lot of climbing and mountaineering. I did most of my climbing towards the end of my break, when I'd finished my Masters. When I first left University I thought I never wanted to go back again, but after a few years of working I became increasingly attracted to doing some further education in the subject that I want to spend the rest of my career in, which is personnel/industrial relations, so I took the Masters. It taught me a lot, it was full time for a year and I got a grant to do it, so it worked out very well. Then I went on a mountaineering expedition to Nepal for a couple of months. I came back to England on the Saturday and started work on the Monday.

People here aren't tremendously impressed or suspicious about the fact that I've taken a career break, they're very neutral and non judgmental about it. I think that if I'd said that I'd wanted to take two years travelling it would have been harder to gain acceptance to get on the Career Break Scheme. I think it would have been perceived by both my boss and the people I came back to work with, as rather more frivolous and not quite what we're looking for from our career minded young personnel managers. So I think the MSc was quite useful in that.

I had been working very hard, but I'd really enjoyed my last job. Taking a break really does rejuvenate you and help you think through your priorities. But it's surprising how quickly you get back into work. I came back to a different job, but I knew a few people here so you pick up with those people quite quickly. You come back with quite a lot of ideas.

The way our Career Break System works is that there is no guaranteed return. We do everything we can to get everyone back into the company, but it's not guaranteed. Most people who have wanted to return have come back. The intention is that they return to the company they came from. I didn't want to go back to my old job, so the obvious next move was for my old boss to look round Unilever for me and keep me in touch with jobs which were coming up. It so happened that at the time I was looking to come back, this job came up in the Head Office. My responsibility is to work with the Personnel Managers and Directors in companies helping them to deliver Equal Opportunities Policies. It's a new job, full time, and I've been here for three months. It's a pretty common progression to move from an operating personnel job into headquarters and back again.

As a man the Career Break Scheme has certainly helped me understand some of the issues for women returning to work after a break from work, getting back in and making contacts again at work. You are sacrificing something about your career, there is a downside to doing it, particularly because of the immediate time out of the business.

The wording of the scheme is quite wide. It includes further education or to care for elderly relatives. There have been one or two males who've been on a career break, but it's predominantly women. Potentially men could also use a career break to look after children or elderly relatives, although there are no examples in Unilever. It's not just attitudes within Unilever, it's attitudes within the whole of society. The whole assumption about taking time off to care is that it is women who do it. So it's pretty rare to challenge that.

Sabbatical leave

Sabbatical leave is a period of time off in addition to annual leave, on full pay, awarded on the basis of length of service. Essentially a sabbatical is a reward for long service which offers the opportunity for employees 'to recharge batteries'. Usually people are entitled to use the leave as they wish; for example a long holiday, voluntary work or more time to pursue a particular interest. It can also be seen as a period in which people can reflect on their careers. Some schemes are of a more limited nature, allowing the leave to be used for a specified purpose, usually educational.

Although there is a tradition of sabbatical leave in the UK in both lecturing and journalism, in general such leave remains fairly rare. Nine men in the survey had taken sabbaticals; three were employed by local authorities, one for a national newspaper, two in the private sector, two for the NHS and one for a church.

Men who are self employed

"I think one of the main reasons organisations are becoming more flexible is because they are leaner and need to take on staff to cover shortfalls without making an employment commitment. I suspect many of the people flexibly employed are in fact contractors."

Managing Director, private company

In *Third Age Careers* authors Curnow and Fox stated their belief that *"a mammoth change in career life is already under way, and companies should recognize that there will be no return to the conventional employment patterns of the 1960s, 1970s or even 1980s – it is too expensive to retain individuals for such a long career span, with all the related costs that this practice entails. Consequently there will be a much more competitive market for core staff, and a greater reliance on short term, contract staff. We are therefore talking about a radical change in a company's future resourcing strategy, which merits attention at the very highest level".*

The NWW survey focused on the issues of flexibility for men who are employed as part of the core workforce in organisations. However three men who returned questionnaires were self employed.

Alan Cockaday previously worked full time for a firm of international consulting engineers and now works on a self employed basis.

❝ *During 1992 I negotiated four months unpaid study leave to complete and submit my PhD. Despite the unwillingness of my immediate line manage to allow study leave, senior management were more supportive and the thesis was successfully completed and awarded in July 1993. In anticipation of the birth of our son (December 1992), I tried to negotiate a more flexible contract. My wife is the Managing Director of a large electronics company and we had always planned that I would be the 'primary home carer' if we had children.*

My immediate line manager was not willing to negotiate a less than full time contract. However, my personnel officer was fully supportive and my claim was heard by senior management and senior personnel. The outcome was unsuccessful as line management insisted that my role could only be fulfilled by a full time member of staff. I then raised the issue of maternity benefits and, in effect, applied for the three year career break available to women within the organisation. Again, immediate personnel were supportive but, it transpired, senior management and/or senior personnel were uncompromising. My application for a 'Paternity Career break' was considered 'not appropriate'.

The only way forward was for me to resign, become self employed and form an indepen-

dent technical consultancy working from home. As I'd just completed a PhD I was well qualified to be a Consultant so it was a good time to launch myself. Life's too short, why work for one company with one set of clients when in a more ideal world you can pick and choose your clients which I do now. Upon doing this, the partnership would 'put me at the top of their list of independent Consultants'. Since 1992 they have continued with our agreement but my involvement has been drastically reduced. However, despite persistent advertising and interviewing, they have only recently managed to recruit my replacement. This replacement took two years to find.

The civil engineering field has gone through a period of intense recession, redundancies and early retirements. Some people work as consultants on a specific three day a week contract. Even though the market has changed my request to work on a more flexible basis seemed quite alien to management. I work at home but the expectation is there that I will be in the office as much as possible. I am currently negotiating further work for another organisation, where I would have to go to their laboratories to work. It was first suggested that I work forty days spread over a year but now it looks as if the post will be around 20-30 hours per week. They were quite concerned that they could only offer the post on a part time basis!

Edward is now two and my workload has averaged at one day per week. I would still expect that to increase, up to three days a week, but I certainly wouldn't hurry back to full time employment and commuting back to London on a regular basis.

Twelve years ago my father would have thought I had made a very foolish move, but now he knows what quality of life is all about and he thinks it's a great thing to do.

Another man who has been working on a freelance/self employed basis as a pensions researcher for five years is supplied with work by his former employer and usually goes into their office two days a week. He comments: *"The issue of being an employee on a service contract or a freelance on a contract for services is not always clear cut. The move from employment to self employment in some organisations has been enforced and viewed simply as a cost-cutting measure. On the other hand, when voluntary, it can be a remarkable way of self-empowerment."*

Chapter four:
Removing barriers to change

"The organisation accepts men job sharing. It does not accept supervisors or managerial job sharing in my opinion."
Team Leader Environmental Management, local authority

On one level the climate for working on a flexible basis seems to be easier and more acceptable for women than for men, mainly because of the enormous numbers of women who work part time (4.6 million) compared to men (0.7 million). Anecdotal evidence from respondents raised several practical issues which have additional implications for men. These focused around finance, negotiating flexible work arrangements and career development. Can organisational cultures change to enable men at senior and managerial levels to alter their working arrangements? In the current culture how do men dare to ask for a flexible arrangement in the first place? And how, if at all do men flourish in a long hours culture when they are no longer part of it? Are colleagues and managers supporting men who wish to or are working on a flexible basis? How can barriers be removed? Some answers (along with more questions) are provided in the following section.

Negotiating the arrangement

"The department I worked for at the time (and the university administration) was hostile to my request. I managed to obtain a position in another department. I had no difficulty when moving to my current department."
Senior Systems Programmer, university

Some organisations, especially local authorities, had well established policies and procedures for negotiating flexible work arrangements. Yet only 34 per cent of respondents acknowledged that they were aware that their organisation had flexible work policies. Sixty six per cent indicated that their organisations did not have policies. Yet some of these individuals worked for local authorities with long recognised policies. In some cases the existence of a policy, even if not well communicated can assist the negotiating process. A lecturer at a university comments: *"There is a job share policy, but I don't think it is very well communicated. I've never seen any bumph going about, but there are quite a few people doing it, people see other people doing it and know it's possible. When we applied to have an official job share there was nothing any-*

one could do about it, as under the organisation's regulations if two people want to job share they can have one."

The private sector tended to rely more on individual arrangements, although some larger companies had policies. A consistent theme emerging was that the higher the value placed on the individual (along with an expressed desire to resign or seek redundancy) the more likely that the employee would receive a sympathetic hearing. This is not surprising considering that 15 per cent of respondents had over ten years service to their organisations.

Sixty one per cent initiated their own arrangement indicating that organisations are listening, if sometimes reluctantly. A General Practitioner in the NHS said that there were *"some suspicions as to why I should want to work half time – some people thought I was a skiver".* Another GP was successful in obtaining a shared post by applying for jobs jointly with his wife. They show that careful preparation previous to interview is part of a successful negotiating process. It is a useful illustration of how to work out communication issues on a day to day basis.

Simon Wilkinson is a GP who job shares with his wife as a partner in a practice in Yorkshire.

❝ *Job sharing only became a possibility for GPs in 1990. Until then you couldn't job share. All GPs work in effect nine sessions a week, that is surgeries, surgery visits and administrative sessions. They have one half day off a week. So full time GPs will work 4.5 days per week plus on call, out of office and night duties as well. GPs are of course self employed. Within our partnership it is up to us how we use our time, subject to agreement with three other partners in the practice who are very flexible.*

My wife and I share half and half, the equivalent of a full time GP's post. I work Mondays and Fridays; Brigit works Tuesdays and Thursdays and we alternate on Wednesdays. On Monday and Friday I do a full day's work from 8:30–6:00. Out of hours work we split between us. It's very straightforward. We had to divide it in a way where we had a reasonable split of time over the week. Patients need to know that there's not a five day gap between when they can come and see you. We are flexible within that. If one of us needed to go off on a course, the other would fill in. We wouldn't do that very often because it wouldn't be fair on the patients.

We manage 11 staff. It's taken the staff a little while to get used to us. The actual day to day management of the staff is done by our Practice Manager who is employed by us. The staff have had to find out where our roles overlap and where they don't overlap. For exam-

ple, they need to know if there's an urgent call with a patient if they can come to me because I'm there instead of Brigit and I'll sort it out. But if it's an administration problem which can wait until the next day then they will ask Brigit.

I had a career break from August 1992 to October 1993. We did voluntary work in India. We went with Action Health, a Cambridge based charity which sends people overseas to projects to train other health workers. In fact that was our first practical experience with job sharing. After some teething trouble we in fact discovered that we could in fact work together. But it wasn't entirely straightforward. We had to sort out our own territories within the work. For example, we couldn't see the same patient at the same time in consultation. It just didn't work. Whilst we inevitably came to the same conclusion about the patient, we came about it from completely different routes. If Brigit was in the clinic that day I was at home writing a teaching plan. That's quite an important thing, particularly for husband and wife job sharers. We ask each other's advice about patients. You do have to set guidelines and you would not interfere with anyone else's management of a patient. You have to set your rules but once you've got that it works extremely well.

We decided to job share before we applied for General Practice posts and applied on a joint CV. Jobs for GPs are advertised in the British Medical Journal as full time partner required. Almost none of the adverts said job share considered. So we applied for a full time vacancy saying we plan to work part time and this is roughly how we will work. I would say perhaps 50 per cent were very positive about it, although they did not fully understand it. Most people when they sit and think about it have actually realized they get far more out of two part timers rather than one full time person. Easily one and a quarter or perhaps one and a half times the work just because if you're not there the next day, then you finish off your paper work, tidy up, and you don't mind so much if you stay that extra hour to work. You probably do more than your fair share of admin. At a practice meeting there is a tendency to actually forget we are only doing one person's job. You just have to watch that a little bit, to make sure you aren't being treated like two full timers.

Brigit was expecting a baby when we were applying for jobs and we said this at interviews. There are no statutory maternity rights when you are self employed so you have to negotiate those. I don't think paternity leave will happen in General Practice. It costs money because you are self employed. As a job sharing couple I don't think we would get maternity and paternity leave at the same time. In some forward looking practices you might find paternity leave is there already. At some point it will become standard practice.

When we were applying for jobs it was really quite interesting how little people knew about job sharing. It really was a shock to quite a lot of doctors who would ask us for example, 'what about holidays, you won't be able to go on holiday together?', the assumption being you can't both take leave from the practice at the same time but of course you can because you're only fulfilling one person's role. People didn't understand that. Or they said, 'won't the patients get confused. They will want to see the doctor on that day they want to see them.' We were not sure if that was going to be a problem but we haven't had any problems at all from the patients. They've really taken to it like ducks to water. They understand entirely that certain days I'm there, certain days Brigit's there, and if they want to know which one of us is there, they ring up.

We decided there was no point having children if you both work full time five days a week and only see them on weekends. I wouldn't have chosen to be a full time house husband because I'd go mad with children all day. One thing practices want to do is to get female doctors into male practices. Women patients want to see women doctors or want to have the option from time to time. Most practices are aware that it's an advantage to them to have a female partner. If you are a female GP you're much more saleable. My biggest asset when applying for jobs was Brigit because she is a female. She might have wanted to stay at home for a year but then she would not have got back into medicine. In the past women have left to have babies. We, if you like, are a good solution to that because our problems of child care are already sorted out within the arrangement.

But from my point of view I get the best of both worlds. I get to spend 2.5 days a week with Anna which is terrific but by the end of those two days I'm also much more enthusiastic about going to work. I'm much less stressed, much less tired. I'm a much better doctor because I can actually sit and listen to people for longer. We could both earn huge amounts of money but then we would have no time in which to spend this extra money. The quality of life is marvellous. I wouldn't swap the money for the free time under any circumstances.

In fourteen per cent of cases the organisation played a role in initiating the flexible working arrangement. A manager in a multinational with 36 years' experience explained to his employer that he wanted more time for religious and pastoral work. The organisation came up with a number of alternatives, including working on a part time basis. He now works 67 per cent of a full time job, including long days which creates the time he needs for pastoral work. Senior staff are divided into two camps, one delighted and supportive, the other puzzled and concerned about commitment. As far as other colleagues are concerned they were used to the fact that he travelled extensively and do not think that his time in the office has changed. Also supervision issues have been overcome.

However, some employers react with surprise, suspicion and hostility. The following comments provide a flavour of some of the difficulties :

"Initial surprise at the proposal. Some scepticism about practicality. The British Medical Association was asked to check the contract."
Consultant in Palliative Medicine

"It was made clear the Headteacher was doing me a favour and that they couldn't guarantee a return to full time work."
Teacher

There was an underlying view emerging that men needed to be more assertive in stating their needs:

"I feel it's a question of making flexible working for men happen (if that's what someone wants) rather than assuming "it can't be done" in our company. My expectation was that the organisation would say no, this isn't possible, and I was wrong. I think that perhaps a lot of men might have the belief there's no point in trying because I know the answer will be no. Well in some cases it might be no, but it might be possible to make something happen, or at least to raise awareness."
Management Trainer, private sector

The following comments highlight the difficulties which can be encountered at local level where the request is for a relatively small change:

"I have been employed by my organisation for 10 years and have held my current position for the last 18 months. I wanted to work more flexible hours so that I could either drop my daughter off at the childminder or collect her and the train times to work meant that I needed to alter my hours in order to do this.

However, when I wanted to negotiate a more flexible pattern of working I experienced great difficulty and the idea met with total negativity from senior staff. Senior management refused to sanction it as it would set a precedent. This, in spite of my line manager agreeing to it in principle. My colleagues too are keen for a more flexible arrangement to be approved for me, but are only vaguely interested in the idea for themselves – most of their wives either don't work or they (male and female) don't have kids yet.

Job share is available for certain jobs within the organisation, but in actual fact the only change I really need to make is to alter either my start or finish time and work either from 8:30 to 4:30, or 9:30 to 5:30, but they are just not interested. I am surprised at the attitude of the Senior Management to my dilemma. However, having said that, sanctioning is a local, not a Human Resources, decision and this no doubt explains the hypocrisy!

Although there are no other posts in the organisation that are worked by men on a flexible basis at least three women in the same office are allowed to do this. In addition, since I made my request, my line manager (single, childless and living with his parents) has been allowed to work from 10.0-5.30 (taking half an hour for lunch instead of 1 hour) as it will save him money on his season ticket!"

The following case history illustrates how the negotiating process should be in an ideal world!

Chris Ashby is an Administrative Officer for the Child Benefit Centre in Newcastle upon Tyne and has three children, aged 23, 14 and 10. He has been working 22 hours, three days a week, Monday–Wednesday since June 1993.

> *Previously I worked full time and altogether I've worked for 15 years. I wanted to spend more time with my family. I have spent a lot of my working life away from them. My wife teaches the youngest at home, so that is the prime reason for my working arrangement.*

Long hours weren't good for me or my family. A few years ago I was in a job where I had to live away from home a lot. I had to travel to Southend and had done that for three years, until we moved. Then I went home for lunch which was great.

Quality of life is very important to me at this stage in my career as I do not see any future promotion prospects. There's no attraction in working full time. When I realised flexible work options were available to me I asked my line manager. Her line manager agreed it. I filled in some paperwork and that was it. From the following Monday I was part time. Also I think it's quite simple to go full time again if necessary.

I think I was more surprised that there wasn't any difficulty from my managers. Not many men work part time and I was a bit nervous to ask. I wondered how they'd see a man working part time, but I didn't have to explain. They said, 'you want to go part time, no problem, what hours do you want, there you are, there's how it will work, and that was it'.

My colleagues took it in their stride. There was an element of muttering but I didn't notice it much at the time. It was perhaps much later on that people approached me and asked why. They were just interested. Men never questioned it at all. My main colleagues just accept it, part and parcel. The children take it in their stride. They would probably get a shock if I worked five days a week. My eldest daughter questions it. She's at university, and she really does many more hours than I do, studying. She has gone on for a PhD and is going to be working at home. I'd like to work from home too. I would be prone perhaps to go full time if I was working at home.

There is now a lot more pressure in the Civil Service. Holidays are more difficult to book, salaries are not as competitive and so flexible working compensates nicely. The equal opportunities policy is great!

Financial implications

"I don't think other staff at my work place understand my motives for working part time, they just see it as a loss of salary, not as a gain in my standard of life."
Instructor, local authority

The loss of immediate income and the effect on pensions do create barriers to working on a flexible basis. A third of respondents mentioned these issues. A sub-editor for a national newspaper states that *"one of the main issues governing job sharing is financial. Many would like to, but feel they can't afford it. For economic reasons I shall be working three instead of two days in 95"*. A lecturer mentioned that *"the only drawback with the pension scheme is that only full time employees can buy added years"*. There are new business opportunities and rewards for those who design pension schemes which attract people working part time. A lead from central government could help to rationalise some of the anomalies in the current pension system.

In many cases where the men had wives or partners the total household income was the most important issue. *"My wife works full time so although it might sound like a big step for me to work three fifths of the week, we've still got 1.6 jobs between us."* Where both partners were working part time and could share the childcare without paying for outside help, there were financial advantages too. *"My wife works part time too and I earn £20,000 a year now, compared with about £33,000 before, but you pay a lot less tax and we don't have to pay for child care, which is extremely expensive. You have to think well 'why am I earning this much money, what is the point, sacrificing time for money?' The driving force was the time and the balance of life and having that time with the children while they are growing up because you know you can always earn more money later on if you want to. Life is about choices, and that is the sacrifice we have to make."*

One man who job shares for a local authority and whose wife works part time thought that *"two jobs are more secure than either of us being full time and the other at home"*.

But finances alter. *"At the beginning it was financially very difficult, but later when we had two half time salaries coming in we seemed very well off, even though it was just the equivalent of just one full time salary. But having said that I'm on the top of a fairly senior scale, so I'm getting £13,000 a year which is perhaps equivalent to the full time salary of someone in another job, so that makes a difference."*

Working flexibly in senior and managerial roles

"It's not so much about men as about the expectations – anyone in a 'senior' job is expected to put the job above all else and work late and at weekends."
Planning Analyst, multinational

A number of men in our survey were working at senior levels and 40 per cent were involved in managing others. The highest full time equivalent salary level was £100,000 and six men were in jobs with full time salaries between £30–60,000. Twenty one were in jobs with salaries between £20–30,000. Some were pleasantly surprised to find that they could reduce hours in a management level job. The following manager found this to be true in his organisation.

Kevin Vickers works part time as Assistant Manager at a London branch of NatWest. He is also a Minister involved in pastoral care and teaching at the Gladstone Mission Evangelical Church in Mitcham.

❝ *I was the first Assistant Manager to work part time in this particular area. I work two days a week, usually Mondays and Fridays, although that is fairly flexible. I started off working full time, then reduced to 18 hours a week, and now work 15 hours a week, in agreement with the Bank.*

I have been attending the Gladstone Mission Evangelical Church for a number of years and I am currently one of the Elders there. Recently I decided to undertake further study, at Spurgeons Baptist Bible College, and attended evening classes whilst on the full time staff at the Bank. I obtained the Cambridge Certificate Qualification which is recognised by the Baptist Ministry. I felt my role at the Church was becoming more and more demanding and discussed this with the Regional Deputy Director at the Bank and it was agreed to reduce my hours to 18 per week.

The branch has around eight full time staff plus part time staff. There is a second in command who knows the job very well. We all have our own in-trays, and we use this system very well as part of the overall communication. I like to organise my time well. I use a filo-

fax and pay a lot of attention to time management. It is one way of coping with the pressures of doing two jobs.

Opinion is valued in discussing how the branch is run and I have a say in management decisions even though I work two days a week. In my particular case, I have no great aspirations about promotion. However there are lots of opportunities now to diversify in the Bank and I don't feel that it would have an adverse affect on promotion if you were working on, perhaps a special project or working as an Assistant Manager within a different department.

The general feeling has been very positive at the branch. We have three part time cashiers coming in as well during the day. I try to be flexible. For example I would come in on the Tuesday after a Bank Holiday and work the Tuesday and the Friday. I still see regular customers who get to know when I am there. Certainly working the Friday and the Monday means that if I meet a customer on a Friday and need to carry on the discussion with them I can simply see them the next working day, which is the Monday. That happened last week with a business customer who was moving premises and wanted a loan to expand her business. What I've been able to do even working part time, for example is, if I dictated a letter and I have needed to sign that letter between the Monday and the Friday, with the centralisation that we have, I can pick the letter up at my home branch, sign it, and send it on. The system works well.

I feel that the arrangement that I have is unique in terms of the Ministry I am able to give in the Church and also to be out there in the real world. It's people that really count. Working part time has been a very positive move.

A Swedish study of *Fatherhood and Corporate Culture* found that some companies were unhappy about men reducing their hours because of fears of seeming unprofessional or uninterested in the customer. If specialists, highly trained individuals, and managers were absent from the job alarm bells were raised about communication and access problems, project delays and more time needed to solve problems. Some mentioned how hard it was for managers to reduce their work hours because of their need to travel, attend meetings and supervise others. Since relations with customers were built on personal relationships, companies felt reluctant to send a customer to another person in the company. However, in reality these very same managers could not always be available for reasons such as family crises, illness, holidays, time out of the office, and meetings.

In Britain there is evidence that attitudes are changing even if the reality may still be confusing. A manager in the private sector acknowledges that in his company *"the need for flexible working arrangements is accepted, but there is very little acceptance that these could apply to senior staff"*. Yet the good news is that men are working at very senior levels in jobs which traditionally would not be viewed as suitable for reduced hours working. The following case history is about two people working reduced hours who as part of a team are on call to provide a sensitive, around the clock response to their terminally ill patients. In addition they use their study time to develop their specialism. It is an inspiring example of what can be achieved at senior levels, in this instance by job sharing.

Andrew Daley is a Consultant in Palliative Medicine for the Sue Ryder Foundation. He job shares with his wife, Rosemary at a Hospice in West Yorkshire.

" *I'm employed as the medical director of the Hospice which means that I am the senior doctor. The Hospice looks after people as in-patients. I also have an advisory role for those at home and in local hospitals. I do quite a lot of teaching, and training as well. The post is full time and I was appointed jointly with my wife. We are equivalent to a Consultant in the hospital where people routinely work 50-60 hours per week. We put in some extra hours because we are able to and it is very difficult trying to keep the hours down.*

Shortly after we got married we decided that we wanted to try job sharing because we were trained in the same way for the same sort of work so we looked around for posts that we thought were suitable and attractive to us. We have two young children (two and a half and nine months old). We have a childminder for the mornings, and then we alternate being responsible for them in the afternoons. It means we see a lot more of the children which is important to us. I used to play a lot of music and job sharing means I am able to continue this interest to some extent.

We have to ensure that one of us is at home to look after the children. Other than that we just swap around and do things as and when. I think on the communication side the organisation and the staff would suffer if we weren't communicating as well as we do. We can spend most of the time over supper talking about what happened in the day, then we stop. There's a lot of informal communication. Most mornings there's actually only one of us here, although we are both working, because one of us is in the hospital, and the other elsewhere. So there's not that much of the time when we are actually both in the building. If we didn't have the opportunity at home to discuss things, it would be difficult.

We both work in the mornings because a lot of the work is actually better done at that time and we alternate being available in the afternoon. In theory neither of us should be working the afternoons, but one of of us is available to work if necessary. So whereas we are sup-

posed to be paid for ten sessions we are actually working thirteen. Just recently we have started taking one morning a week each off. But then that doesn't count the paper work we do in the evenings. Attending meetings makes it difficult to keep to a set work pattern. For example, it's impossible to say that I will always work Monday afternoons and Rosemary will always work Tuesday afternoons. We need to be flexible because a lot of the committees and bodies that we sit on prefer that one of us take on a particular responsibility.

There isn't any clear promotion model for us. When you are appointed as a Consultant there isn't really anywhere above that to go. There are very few people who are job sharing at this level and once you are appointed as consultant it's quite unusual to move. In general in the hospital system when you are appointed you stay there for the rest of your career. We were clear in the contract that we both had to have a reasonable amount of study leave built in.

I think it would be very difficult to do this post full time, on my own. Certainly in the long term, because of the kind of work that we are doing. It's quite emotionally demanding with patients dying and it does worry us as to what effect it will have on us over ten years, twenty years. From that point of view we think it is important to have time away and hopefully develop our own interests.

We are in the NHS pension scheme, even though the Sue Ryder Foundation is not part of the NHS. If the spouse dies, their partner only gets half of the pension in the NHS scheme. As that personal pension is going to be half of the normal one because of working part time, it comes down to a quarter and that is worrying. In general we are lucky that the salary is sufficient so that we don't feel the need to earn more money. In that sense we are financially secure.

I think people have been very pleased with how the shared post has worked and I think they see it as a great success and an asset. I think that our employers would be open if someone else wanted to jobshare in the future. Friends are generally very interested and positive. Some medical friends are envious. A lot of doctors marry other doctors, but there are very few people who marry within the same specialism. Apart from GPs (and there are a number of GPs who job share) I don't know of any other specialists who do. I think they would like to be able to do the same thing. And we have a reasonable balance in life. We would like to get a little bit more control of our time. That is coming slowly. You can't ever feel properly balanced and in control because of the unpredictable nature of the job. We are on call every week day and every fourth weekend.

The range of experience and achievements of the participants should prompt more board level reviews as to whether other senior posts in organisations might benefit from new working patterns. One participant sums it up neatly:

"I wondered about job sharing. There is a senior manager who is a friend of mine, who has similar views, and although he has a partner who doesn't work, he does try very hard to get home. It has crossed my mind that if we could establish a job share in what is regarded as a senior job, then that would be a tremendous breakthrough."

Career development and progression

"I think working part time has had no effect one way or the other on my promotion prospects. The first time I applied I didn't get it, the second time I did – but that's fairly standard. I'm now going to try for another promotion and this will be quite a difficult jump."
Senior Systems Programmer, university

Fifty-three per cent of men surveyed were positive about their promotion prospects. This may be due to increased enthusiasm for work, better time management, clear objectives and increasing confidence to seek promotion on a flexible basis.

Forty-eight per cent of men were negative about their promotion prospects and some of the dissatisfaction was due more to the career patterns of their profession rather than flexible working itself. A Solicitor who job shares sets out career progression in the legal profession:

"In the law the normal pattern is that you start as an assistant and that you look for and find a partnership, and work your way up a partnership. The first thing is that doing a job share I am not looking for a partnership, so that progression is on ice. The second thing is that there is an assumption that people should find a partnership within a number of years of qualifying. There is no fixed time – but really the sooner the better. The longer I leave it before getting a partnership or setting up on my own the more suspicious people will be about why I haven't done it sooner. All I am doing is reflecting the prejudices of the profession. I can see realistically that what I am doing could have a negative effect on my career. Whether it will – whether I will overcome the problems remain to be seen. The point about a partnership is that you take a percentage of the profits. What you would do is have a lower percentage of the profits. The only thing a partner might say is that if you are not there full time you are not taking a full share of the administrative responsibilities. But that is reflected in the reduced share of the profits. I have heard of people who are part time partners."

What other issues affect promotion? Delayering, widespread redundancies, and the collapse of the conventional career mean that some men discover their own "glass ceiling" and are prepared to opt out of the system, if only on a temporary basis. Some men have decided (as many women have) that they do not want to progress further in their career because the personal cost is too high. Quality of life and the desire for a life outside work moves up the agenda. The need for a pause in a career is expressed by a Divisional Deputy Director at a University who says that *"I think that flexible working is extremely beneficial for my relationship with my children at a key stage in their development, but is a bad move, temporarily, for my career. Obviously I have struck a good bargain"*. Traditional assumptions about careers and career success can create barriers and there is a recognition that there is a downside to increased responsibility. A University Lecturer states that *"I know quite a lot of people who've been promoted, but don't like it"*.

A man working part time in the private sector commented that *"from my point of view I was aware that if I chose to work part time, I would be sending out signals that I wanted more balance so this would not unreasonably be seen as limiting my career prospects. Now in fairness, this hasn't worried me, because I don't want to be promoted, as I'm quite happy where I am. I wouldn't want to be the next level up because you are much more of an administrator"*.

Organisations assume that everyone wishes to follow similar career paths. However, this does not take into account the realities of day to day life. Employees reluctantly shape their behaviour and ambitions in accordance with those of the organisation. Individuals feel pressured to sacrifice balance in their lives because they also want to progress in their careers. A General Manager for a multinational states that *"For men or women, it seems to me that flexibility is incompatible with ambition in an international company. It is applicable if either ambition is satisfied (as in my case) or temporarily abandoned (as in starting a family)."*

Taking a career break is clearly going to affect promotion prospects in the short term. In a large organisation which does have a fairly predictable career ladder a Personnel Officer thinks that *"there is a perception that to step out of the normal career progression is something quite unusual for a man, also, that's why we've had so many issues about trying to remove some of those barriers for women. But those sorts of things don't fit in with an old fashioned part of the culture, which is still there and for a male stepping out it is quite unusual"*.

Attitudes of colleagues

"As a widower with two young daughters I think I get more tolerance and support than most single parents."
Welfare Rights Officer, local authority

"Most of the women are very supportive. I have no idea how senior men view me. I think a lot of prejudice is mitigated by how well you are perceived to do your job."
Departmental Systems Officer, local authority

The majority of men reported positive attitudes towards their working arrangement from other staff with comments such as 'supportive' and 'accepting'. If a member of staff is perceived to be contactable, then the attitude of staff tends to be positive. A Chief Technical Specialist in the private sector comments that *"there can be minor frustration when problems occur and I am not there. Everyone is happy so long as communication is working properly. They are secure in the knowledge I could be contacted if necessary, and I will respond positively"*.

A Senior Systems Programmer at a university expressed the view that *"they recognise the benefit of having two half time people. As with any job there is pressure to get things done and sometimes people have to wait longer if only one of us can deal with a particular problem"*.

Men felt that women were very understanding. A Managing Director of a private company states that his colleagues (both women with older children) were supportive. An Economic Policy Adviser for a local authority says that *"some think it's good that a man takes looking after his children seriously"*. Julian Duxfield, who took a two year career break from Unilever commented that *"the reaction from women has been 'here's a man who's done a similar thing to me' and it's just that you've both sacrificed a career move to do something else"*.

But reactions vary. A Landscape Assistant at a local authority says his colleagues *"like it because it works. Sometimes they are envious because they don't see the homework. I tend to try to fit a week's work into 3 days as most of the people around me are full timers."* A Volunteer Coordinator who works part time 20 hours per week summarises the paradox as follows:

"Some appreciate the fact that I do other things away from my paid work – but only those that know me. Others seem to think that I breeze into the office whenever I like. C'est la vie!"

Some men felt marginalized. A Neighbourhood Coordinator in a local authority said that *"when I job shared I felt that I was specifically marginalized as a 'part timer' of proportional less importance. This came from both male and female colleagues"*.

Others felt vulnerable, particularly when deadlines had to be met. A Principal Social Worker declares that *"there is a tendency to expect me to be in work 37 hours a week although I get paid for 18.5 hours!"* And other factors such as delays in recruiting or unfilled halves of jobs can make a team feel negatively about flexible working when the issue is really not about the method of working.

Attitudes of senior staff

"I think that at higher levels they are of the view that if people are comfortable in the work-place, and are achieving, they are happy. I think they would much rather have me work-ing part time and happy and contributing, than forcing me to work full time and resenting it and not performing."
Management Trainer, private sector

"Positive and supportive. I'm also lucky to be working for an organisation that is very keen on helping employees with childcare arrangements."
Press and Publicity Officer, voluntary organisation

Balanced Lives confirms that people and organisations can accommodate change on an individual basis. An organisation benefits from a motivated and committed employee. A Principal Trading Standards Officer in a local authority says management *"know when I will be at work in any given week and that if the job demands I can be contacted at home and will work different or extra hours"*. And a Welfare Rights Officer from a local authority is convinced that senior management *"think they get more work out of me"*.

Yet some senior staff remain ambivalent, wanting staff to be present at all times. A Principal Building Surveyor for a local authority indicates *"acceptance but they would have preferred it not to have happened,"* while a principal social worker says there is *"disappointment when I'm not due to work"*. A Divisional Deputy Director at a University who works 3.5 days indicates that management is *"reasonable, perhaps slightly more critical than colleagues"*.

The distance that some senior managers maintain in organisations can work favourably for those who are seeking to change their working arrangements on the ground. A view from a man who works in the private sector is that "the amount of communication we have with our senior managers is quite limited anyway, so there haven't been any comments".

Culture change

"The culture 'on high' in personnel departments is probably very receptive. The biggest resistance, however, is at a 'cultural' level in the office and amongst work colleagues whose own career priorities affect their judgement of how well you perform."
Volunteer Coordinator, local authority

"As the only man in this office (only two in the whole organisation) the culture had already changed to favour women working part time for childcare reasons."
Information and Publicity Officer, voluntary organisation

Organisational culture is the characteristic spirit and belief of an organisation, demonstrated, for example, in the norms and values that are generally held about how people should behave and treat each other, the nature of working relationships that should be developed and attitudes to change. These norms are deep, taken for granted, assumptions, which are not always expressed and are often known about without being clearly understood. It is important that those employed in an organisation should try to understand the culture they share. Full time working is a central part of the culture of most organisations.

Yet this survey has identified certain inroads in some cultures particularly in local authorities. A Principal Trading Standards Officer states that he is *"not aware of men being treated any differently to women who work part time"*. A Divisional Services Manager in a local authority agrees that the culture is changing and that *"more men are doing this for personal/career reasons"*. A contrary view expressed by a Principal Building Surveyor who took a 12 month career break is that *"there is a certain apathy which means that people are not very concerned by it as an issue"*. A Principal Employee Development Officer in a local authority says the culture has not changed and that there is an *"assumption that despite working a job share, I'll nevertheless be available to cover at non-contracted working times"*.

Cultures can vary between different parts of an organisation as pointed out by a training co-ordinator, in a local authority: *"I don't think that there was ever a time when it wasn't acceptable for men to work less than full time in this organisation – certainly not in the time that I've been working there. People may disagree with it in private, but they certainly don't express those views publicly, so there is no lack of 'acceptability'. Having said that, I don't think that job sharing is open to manual operatives, and so this represents a large section of the organisation where part time working for men is not accepted (most operatives being male). I think that part time working for men is far more accepted in the public sector than amongst private sector employers."*

This is a significant comment. It was difficult to find men in manual jobs to interview to discover their experiences of flexible working. The culture needs to change in both private and public sectors to include the needs of and aspirations of all men.

Within the twenty four hour culture of health care there were notes of optimism expressed by a General Practitioner in the NHS who said *"now they see the system works they can see it has advantages, I'm less tired at work and more enthusiastic"*. A Consultant in Palliative Medicine who job shares with his wife says that *"it was not considered unacceptable – just unusual"*.

Many men who work flexibly in organisations are the exception rather than the norm. *"I think I'm very much an anomaly. On a small scale, I believe that the longer I'm there and seen to be effective the culture may be influenced bit by bit"* says a Youth Worker from a local authority. A Senior Technician at a local authority who works 18.5 hours a week says that *"as far as I know there are only two men working part time. The other was recruited as part time whereas I changed from full time. Male colleagues have expressed envy at my working hours and would like to follow suit. To date none have taken any action, though finance restricts some"*.

Evidence of culture change in the private sector is also patchy. A Manager in the private sector states that *"flexible working is available equally to all employees, male or female, full and/or part time, subject to fitness for purpose"*. An Employee Development Manager in the private sector says that it would be *"acceptable in very junior jobs, clerical or secretarial for example. But not for a male who wanted a career progression"*. A Planning Analyst who leaves work most days at 4:30pm to collect the children is adamant that quite the opposite is happening and that *"as we lay people off, those still in work are expected to work longer hours and be available at weekends etc"*. For those edging towards retirement the view from a General Manager, Finance and Human Resources, is that organisational culture is more accommodating and flexible working is *"more likely for pre-retirement than earlier in a career"*. His view is mirrored by a Manager for a technical consultancy that although the culture is changing, *"most can't afford it. I am aware of another employee who is negotiating 'gradual retirement' via part time work"*.

"My personal view is that there hasn't been a culture change. Although the policy of the organisation as an Equal Opportunities employer is to provide Career Break opportunities for men, career minded men will still need to be in full time employment."
Graduate Assessor/Interviewer, private sector

Although change is slow, some men feel that where their arrangements work well, this is part of the process which brings about changes within the culture. A solicitor says that *"the partners are very positive about it. They've seen that it can work and they understand how it works and they've seen good results from it, so I'm sure they would consider it for someone else. Since we've joined, they've started considering women who've had children and who are coming back for one or two days a week. One of the other solicitors has negotiated an arrangement where she has every Wednesday off so she's gone down to a four day week. Maybe these things would have happened anyway, but my guess is that their willingness to try these arrangements stems from the fact that they've seen it working so well with us".*

A Danish Study found that there is one particularly significant difference between departments taking a positive view of the priority men give to their children and those which are more reserved or negative. In a workplace with no competition between employees, where people work in groups or team, the environment is positive. When the career structure favours direct or indirect competition between employees, it is more likely to be hostile.

Men in organisations are willing to work longer hours, meet tight deadlines, travel extensively, participate in residential training courses and move house at the behest of the company if they want to rise to the highest levels of organisations. These work demands are likely to be incompatible with domestic responsibilities. Men in junior and senior management frequently depend upon the support of wives to manage all domestic and familial matters and for many men this support is no longer there. The search for the 'happy family' in employment may be at the cost of an increasingly unhappy family in the domestic sphere.

In the end culture can be about empowerment. A Youth Worker for a local authority sums it up as follows:

"For me it's about culture. It never occurred to me that I could work anything other than full time (although I've worked bizarre and sometimes flexible hours for several years) until it was staring me in the face. Now I'm not sure that I'd consider full time work (whatever that is). Deciding on a different way of working has been about positive choice and taking control. I now feel much more in control of what I do in my family life and in my work life."

Chapter five:
Men, Paternity and Parental Leave

The International Year of the Family in 1994 focused attention on a range of working practices and employer support designed to enhance family life, including the need for the introduction or improvement of leave arrangements for male and female staff, such as paternity, parental and family leave.

As a result many employers have re-examined their stance on family friendly issues. For example Business Sectors within the NatWest Group are currently enhancing and broadening their flexible leave arrangements to reflect changing staff needs while meeting their business objectives.

A Group Flexible Leave Framework has been developed encompassing core Group values and standards and business objectives whilst providing guidance for leave schemes.

The Framework principles have been designed to reflect:
- business demand for increasing flexibility in the workplace
- statutory and sociological developments
- best practice in Human Resources policies and procedures

The Framework brings together and enhances existing temporary leave arrangements throughout the Group. A wider choice of flexible options for staff is included to help reconcile work and external commitments of a temporary nature, for example, leave to meet caring responsibilities, adoption leave, emergency leave, paternity leave (eg five days paid leave and additional discretionary leave), study and travel leave.

The emphasis is on creating maximum flexibility to meet both business objectives and staff needs, aiding recruitment, retention and development of staff and to ensure NatWest make full use of all talent available.

Paternity leave in the UK

Many employers in the UK do offer paternity leave, paid or unpaid, as an extra benefit and see it as a good business move which enables them to maintain competitive terms and conditions. A survey of 356 UK companies carried out in 1994 by Industrial Relations Services found that the costs of such schemes are minimal amounting to the equivalent of 23 minutes per employee per year. Reasons given for offering such leave vary, but in many cases it is seen as an integral part of an equal opportunities programme.

Of the 356 organisations surveyed, 245 (69 per cent) had paternity leave arrangements. In all but two cases, the leave was paid. Most of the employers, three quarters, offer the leave as a contractual right, and in the other quarter it is at management discretion. Three fifths introduced paternity leave after 1990 and the most common reason was equal opportunities. Many of the reasons given reflected a growing awareness of the important role both parents play at the birth of a child and the need to balance home and work responsibilities. British Gas introduced paternity leave *"as part of a new package of terms and conditions which contained improved career support to enable men and women to combine work and family responsibilities"*. Uniroyal Englebert Tyres considered it to be 'a social duty'. Some, like Argos, mentioned 'to maintain competitive terms and conditions'.

There was a wide variation in the time allowed for example from one day at ABB Transportation and Strathclyde Regional Council, to 20 days at BECTU, the media trades union. There was also variation in whether additional leave was granted and in what circumstances and whether it was paid or not. Some employers limit the frequency of the leave to once a year and there were also differences about when the leave had to be taken. Some employers specified the time had to be taken at or around the time of birth, others allowed more flexibility of timing. For example Brent Council and The Children's Society both permit leave to be taken between 11 weeks before and up to 52 weeks after the birth. This flexibility can extend to allowing the choice of taking the leave as a whole block or in separate parts.

Requirements

Most of the employers (63 per cent) did not require a minimum length of service in order to qualify. Of those that did, it varied from three months length of service to two years. The most common requirement, where one existed, was twelve months. Around half of respondents extended paternity leave to adoptive parents and a further nine per cent had a separate adoption leave policy. Most took their employees leave on trust. Two thirds did not insist on documentary evidence, but about half required notice of intention to take it.

Since introducing their paternity leave scheme about 16 per cent have made improvements, mostly in respect of the length of leave and also to include 'partners' as well as 'spouses', paid leave instead of unpaid, adoptive leave or the abolition of service requirements. Schemes negotiated by trades unions seemed to result in longer leave entitlement, (a median length of five days as opposed to three where there was no union agreement). However five days still falls short of the official TUC recommendation to seek 10 days paternity leave.

Other European countries provide the following statutory entitlements to paternity leave.

- Denmark: 10 days leave to be taken during the first 14 weeks paid on same basis as maternity leave
- Belgium: three days leave paid at 100 per cent of earnings
- Spain: two days paid at 100 per cent of earnings
- France: three days to be taken during the 15 days before and after the birth
- Sweden: two weeks at 80 per cent of earnings
- Finland: one week at 66 per cent of earnings during the maternity or the parental leave periods
- Statutory paternity leave is also available in Norway (two weeks unpaid)

Men's views on paternity leave
"Paternity leave and greater support for men as carers are needed."
Senior Library Assistant, local authority

The men who were interviewed were unanimous about the importance of paternity leave. Few worked in organisations with formal paternity leave arrangements, but many had made use of special leave, paid or unpaid to take time off at the time of birth. A trainer in the private sector feels that *"paternity leave is vital. Most people take a fortnight's holiday. I think it's scandalous because when you have a new baby it's such an emotional time, a time of huge transition, for the individual and the family. I think you need the partner to be there, in a practical sense to help and support and come to terms with their own feelings about what's happened and just to get to know this baby, this new person".*

A worker in the voluntary sector states that *"for me paternity leave is crucial in order to have a lot of time off around the birth of my children. When my first child was born I was a student nurse, I was in training and went to my manager to ask what arrangements there were to have time off when my baby was born. He said you get three days off if something goes wrong. I took sick leave when the baby was born and told them in advance I was going to. When I wanted three weeks I went to my doctor and asked for a sick note. When he asked what's the matter, I said I'm a new father. He said that's not an illness. I said it is preventative mental health care and you need to sign me off sick or I'll go a bit mad if I'm at work when my child is born. So he did it and said it was necessary for me to have time away from work. Nobody asked any questions about it. So I've actually engineered a combination of sickness and taking holidays, my own home made paternity leave. It's one of the special times of your life. If you miss out on it, it's really hard to get that back somehow, you miss out on this very powerful time. I think men suffer as a result. They become so distant from the experience".*

Parental leave

Parental Leave is time off work for either parent following or including the end of maternity leave, to care for a young child.

As families with young children are often under financial pressure, fathers in these families tend to work more than other men. In Sweden, men frequently say they do not take Parental Leave because they are afraid of their employer's reaction, but several reports have shown their worries are often exaggerated. Fathers do however need active encouragement from their employers to take leave and there are many ways in which this can be done, such as promoting bosses who take leave and giving extra support to small employers who do have problems when workers take leave. For example, a Swedish insurance company has a programme to encourage men to take Parental Leave, which offers every man and woman a cash bonus if they stay at home for at least six weeks, and a recent report shows that more men have been encouraged to take leave as a result of this programme.

The Parental Leave Directive

The European Commission Parental Leave Directive was first proposed in 1983. At that time its main feature was a minimum unpaid leave period of three months per worker per child. This would mean that in a two parent family where both parents are at work there would be a total entitlement of at least six months to be equally divided between parents. However both parents may not be on leave at the same time, nor is the leave entitlement transferable from one parent to the other. The directive was intended to establish common statutory provisions throughout the EU, to guide already developing provisions on extended leave and to make sure that these were non discriminatory. It was argued that the introduction of such a leave system would promote the welfare of children and help parents combine work and family commitments.

The introduction of parental leave with a period specifically included for the father would give recognition to and encourage the role of the father in childcare. Because the UK already allows for 40 weeks' maternity leave for women, the directive would not have affected our provisions for women to have time off work to care for babies. However the UK makes no statutory provision for men and this is where the directive would affect the UK. The UK Government opted out of the 1983 Directive, which is currently being redrafted by the European Commission and widened to incorporate a more constructive approach to the reconciliation of professional and family life.

Parental leave in other European countries

Eight of the European Union countries already have a statutory right to parental leave of varying kinds, giving parents the right to return to work at the end. In France three years is allowed, unpaid unless there are more than three children in the family. Denmark allows 10 weeks at 90 per cent of earnings, Belgium and Germany allow 18 months paid at a flat rate, and Spain gives 12 months unpaid leave. The important point about parental leave is that it can be taken by either parent, or shared between the two. The UK has the longest amount of maternity leave at 40 weeks (mainly unpaid). However, when the provisions for parental leave and maternity leave are looked at together, it is clear that Britain lags behind most other countries in the length of leave allowed, the payment of it and by only providing for mothers.

By providing for either parent to take statutory parental leave a government is not only giving choice to the parents; it is taking a lead in encouraging men to be more involved with their children. We know from statistics that even in countries where there is a statutory right to take time off with children, it is still overwhelmingly women who take it up. This is partly down to tradition, but must mainly reflect the fact that women's earnings are normally less than men's. Even in Sweden this is true – but the Swedish government have recently grasped this nettle. In June 1994 the Swedish parliament passed a law requiring fathers to take a month of the government paid child care leave, or lose a month of the benefit. One month of leave is allocated specifically to fathers.

Parental Leave in the UK

The Cooperative Bank announced a new agreement for its 1,500 male staff in September 1994. It follows the provisions of the parental leave directive and will allow up to three months unpaid leave for fathers. Mr Terry Thomas, the Bank's Managing Director said when interviewed by the *Financial Times* that *"in the future when we come to determining appropriate conditions of employment for staff we will be looking more to European cooperative banks than to our rivals in this country"*. He added that the cost of the leave to the bank would be marginal. The Bank will meet the pension contributions of staff on leave and use contract workers to fill the vacancies.

Family Leave

Family leave is short-term leave to enable working parents to take time off when children have an accident or suffer illness and the usual care arrangements break down. Other reasons could include the illness of a disabled member of the household, clinic appointments and medical treatment, and the death or illness of a close relative. Parents enjoy a statutory right to family leave in five European countries: these are Belgium, Germany, Greece, Portugal and Spain.

Family leave entitles employees to a minimum number of days of paid leave each year. Special leave that is currently available to many employees may meet some, but often does not meet all, of these needs, and its availability can also be limited by discriminatory assumptions about family roles. Proper provision for family leave reduces the possibility of discriminatory provision of special leave and enables family obligations to be recognised and discussed. This can reduce tension and strain in the workplace and also reduce absenteeism. Family leave of five days was recommended by the recent Employment Select Committee Report *'Mothers in Employment'*.

Chapter six:
The international perspective

The experience in other countries reveals some interesting experiments as to how men can balance work and domestic life. The European Commission (EC) is funding The Families and Work Network for three years. This initiative brings together those concerned with ways of improving the balance between family life and the world of work. New Ways to Work has been chosen as the lead body in the UK. The EC is also looking at ways to promote men's involvement in caring for children in the workplace, in leave arrangements and to place and support male workers in services for young children.

Sharing the load in Australia

In Australia the Federal Government set up a communication education campaign – Working Families: Sharing the Load – conducted by the Office on the Status of Women within the Department of the Prime Minister, and initiated after Australia ratified ILO Convention 156, "Workers with family responsibilities" in 1990. The aim of the programme is to *"enable workers with family responsibilities, who are employed or wish to be employed, to do so without discrimination and, as far as possible, without conflict between their employment and their family responsibilities"*. The government also has a Work and Family Unit which has developed a strategy for implementing the convention across Commonwealth policies and programmes.

Gender equality in Sweden

For more than 25 years Sweden has had an official policy of gender equality. However, this goal has not been reached. While Swedish women are almost as likely to be in the labour force as men, they occupy a narrower range of jobs and at lower pay. Many mothers prefer to work part time, in order to cope with home and family responsibilities, and a majority of Swedes still feel that men are more responsible than women for providing family income. Men continue to be more committed to employment than family life, work full time, spend less hours doing housework than women, and while very active in child care, leave primary responsibility for children to their partners. While almost half of all fathers take parental leave, mothers still take 91 per cent of all days available. Although by law Swedish fathers have access to a wide array of benefits which allow them to stay at home to care for their children, most fathers working for the largest private corporations are not taking full advantage of these benefits.

With this background in mind, Linda Haas and Philip Hwang collected data from Swedish companies which in turn raised issues about the gendered culture of work organisations. This is reflected in 'family friendly' policies which may on the exterior be for all, but in reality efforts are directed towards women with few employers expecting men to take advantage of such policies. Their study found that Swedish companies are generally aware of work family issues as they involve men and offer at least some formal or informal support to fathers. But few have undertaken widescale changes in corporate policy and practice that would make the work environment highly supportive of active fatherhood, and men's use of leave benefits in these companies is modest.

They found that the least used family leave benefit of all is fathers' right to reduce work hours. While the majority of companies say at least one father has done this, only a small percentage of fathers in their company (less than ten per cent) had participated in this program. No company indicated that 20 per cent or more of their fathers had reduced work hours. These numbers are in marked contrast to Swedish women. Two-thirds of women living in a household with a male partner and at least one child work part time. Only eight per cent of the companies surveyed said that more fathers were asking to reduce work hours in comparison to the previous years, while most (87 per cent) said the numbers were constant. This is not surprising, given the negative attitudes towards this benefit expressed by employers in the survey. Over three quarters said more fathers reducing work hours would cause 'some' or 'big' problems, while only five per cent said it would not cause problems.

Paternity leave/parental leave in Denmark

There are two categories of statutory leave for fathers in Denmark:
- Paternity leave: two weeks leave reserved for the father during the first 14 weeks after birth.
- Parental leave: The parents' joint entitlement to leave in the 15th-24th weeks after the birth. This leave can be divided freely between the parents, although they may not take it concurrently and it must be taken for whole days.

In 1985 approximately 41 per cent of new fathers used their entitlement to paternity leave, while about three per cent used their right to parental leave. The equivalent figures for 1991 were around 55 per cent and approximately three per cent. Today, just over half of all fathers take parental leave. Most attention is still paid to men's continuing low use of the long parental leave scheme. Why do fathers not take parental leave?

A survey of leave conditions with regard to children born in the period 1984-1989 sought to find the answer to this question. Independently of their partners, parents were asked to state the most significant reason for the father not having taken parental leave. Mothers more often gave breastfeeding as a reason and fathers the high financial cost for the family. These two aspects are among the most important reasons for a family deciding to let the mother take all the parental leave. With regard to breastfeeding, the official recommendation of the Danish National Board of Health is that, if possible, the child should be breast fed for six months in order to build up the necessary immunities and to prevent any later allergies. For parents choosing to follow this recommendation it is difficult for the father to take parental leave, since the six month breastfeeding period corresponds to the total leave entitlement after childbirth.

Financial considerations continue to be a large barrier to men taking parental leave. Even though public-sector employees won entitlement to full salary during leave in 1989 this has primarily been to the woman's benefit, since mothers are more likely than fathers to be public employees. Surveys show that if the father is employed in the private sector, and because of the general discrepancy between women's and men's salary levels, the loss of income is lower if the mother takes leave than if the father were to take parental leave. It can thus be assumed that in up to 70 per cent of families the loss of income in connection with parental leave is higher if the father rather than the mother takes the parental leave.

There are other significant grounds for fathers not taking parental leave. Firstly, there are still many families who consider children to be the primary responsibility of the mother. Secondly, parental leave was prevented by the father's work. It has long been suspected that the father's work is one of the greatest impediments to his taking leave in connection with paternity. This has been confirmed by recent surveys in the Nordic countries. However, there has been a lack of more detailed knowledge of this factor. One issue is the extent to which senior personnel communicate to their staff that it would be inappropriate for a father to take leave. It is possible that other factors play a larger role, for example the importance of work to men's identity.

A survey in 1989 found that in a male-dominated workplace, all male employees considered parental leave to be a good idea, but they also all believed that their colleagues were against men taking parental leave. Instead there is a trend for fathers to save up time off in lieu of overtime and holiday leave, which they use to extend their paternity leave. Some men planned in great detail how they could get extra time off, for example by doing a lot of overtime during their partner's pregnancy. It should be noted that this absence from work is not recorded as childbirth-related leave. (This section draws from *The Equality Dilemma* by Carlsen and Larsen.)

USA

In her book *Breaking the Mold*, Lotte Bailyn refers to work which was being carried out in 1993 by several teams of researchers, with support from the Ford Foundation. They worked with companies to reconsider the way they think about work in order to help them be productive and competitive and still allow their employees to meet their personal needs. Though the results of this effort are not yet known, these researchers have discovered how difficult it is for company officials even to agree that employees personal lives are or should be of concern to their employers. As a member of the human resource department at one of these companies explained *"for over a decade we have tried to teach managers to ignore employees' private circumstances. So it's not easy to get them to think about these issues in a different way"*.

The debate in America is a cultural one. What is a 'good' father? Can he be both provider and nurturer within the context of the workplace where long hours and unstated assumptions about appropriate behaviour dominate? Men experience an 'invisible dilemma', the same work-family conflicts as mothers but it is invisible because they do not talk about it openly.

Americans have tended to focus on corporate programmes to help employees balance work and family responsibilities and once again most programmes seemed to be in response to the needs of working mothers. A highly influential book published in 1987, *Workforce 2000*, indicated some dramatic demographic changes, including the fact that white males would be a minority of new entrants to the labour force by the year 2000. In 1990 the Harvard Business Review published an article by R.R. Thomas entitled *'From affirmative action to affirming diversity'*. This explored the fundamental principles on which much equal opportunities work is based and presented a different way. Kandola and Fullerton have written fully about diversity initiatives in *Managing the Mosaic* and use the following working definition:

"The basic concept of managing diversity accepts that the workforce consists of a diverse population of people. The diversity consists of visible and non-visible differences which will include sex, age, background, race, disability, personality and workstyle. It is founded on

the premise that harnessing these differences will create a productive environment in which everybody feels valued, where their talents are being fully utilised, and in which organisational goals are met."

In *Men as Carers* the diversity movement was commended as *"one of the most important workplace initiatives in the US: …(while) paying attention to 'new groups' joining the workforce, our diversity programmes largely ignore that there has been a growing value shift among (working fathers)".*

To challenge this idea, Jim Levine has begun identifying the best companies for working fathers, publishing them annually in a parent magazine; his top choice is a Fathering Programme run at the Los Angeles Department of Water and Power, which was introduced by a woman executive to increase productivity. *"I would like to see us discussing family friendly companies with an understanding that family means mother and father (but) for now the identification of 'father friendly' companies is a necessary transitional step …(otherwise) 'family friendly' will keep getting interpreted as mother friendly".*

Experience from other countries indicates the value of role models, diversity of approach, and monitoring and evaluating programmes to ensure that today's solution is not tomorrow's problem.

Chapter seven:
Men and the future of work

What is the future of work? Is it longer hours for the few? Will employers organise on a different basis to devise structures and measures that accommodate individual needs? And what about the growth of information technology? The view from the experts indicates that change of an unpredictable nature will continue but that it can also provide opportunities for those wishing to do so to work in new ways.

Charles Handy writes in *The Empty Raincoat* that *"young people, in particular, face a world very different from the one their parents grew up in, a world where there are not very many models from the past for them to draw on, where they really do have to reinvent their lives, their purposes and their standards and their priorities"*. Sir Iain Vallance, Chairman of British Telecom, continues that theme by saying that *"the turbulence and change which managers currently face across all UK industries is unprecedented ... things are going to continue to change. No question. Secondly, the pace of change will continue to accelerate ... to build a career in the future – and a career in which working for several organisations will become the norm – they must become 'knowledge workers', capable of using the vast amount of information that modern technology will make available to them"*. Sir Iain calls for the workforce to *"manage the unexpected"* and to anticipate change.

Some men are very clear that the conventional career structure is no longer relevant for them. A training officer for a local authority explains:

"I think there is a general difficulty in understanding that just because a man is working for a large organisation he's not necessarily going to make it his career. There is insufficient recognition of the fact that people do not enter organisations at 16 and have a job for life any more. I don't think that men who work less than full time are taken so seriously as those who do when it comes to career progression. I imagine that the situation in the private sector (in which I have also worked) would be much worse than this, and I can understand the comment that part time male workers are 'seen as eccentrics'. There is less take up of flexible work options by men because the traditional image of men as breadwinners and careerists is still very strong."

Mike Whitaker opted to retire at the age of 53 as a managerial grade Civil Servant and care for his daughters who are six and four years old. He has developed a portfolio of part time occupations. He writes and illustrates magazine articles, works as a Redundancy Counsellor and benefits advisor, trained as a Lay School Inspector and is writing the second draft of a novel. He wrote to New Ways to Work to say that *"in the future our working lives will mix 'n' match – there will be some employment, some self employment, some full time, some part time. Sometimes work will involve going out, sometimes it will be done at home – teleworking, perhaps. Sometimes the man will work, sometimes the woman. People will leave work earlier (they are already – I believe the average age of 'retirement' is down to about 55) as indeed they should if they have a pension they can draw. Why should spouses not job share? Why should older men with younger working wives not reverse roles? But all of that will entail an enormous shift in attitudes, especially amongst men, both at the top and at shopfloor level".*

He has made the shift to a life where each day is different and fulfilling.

Concern about unemployment

"Job sharing is a lifestyle commitment for me. Our society would be a much better place to live in if there was no unemployment, less material greed etc."
Team Leader, Environmental Management, local authority

A number of men had strong views on the fact that we are becoming a society where some people are working long hours with the resultant stress which this brings whilst others are unemployed and living in poverty. A trainer in the private sector said that *"what seems to happen is that organisations want to reduce the staff and put more demands on those that remain, and then you just have a whole host of people who are out of work, and it just seems crazy to me".*

A number of men stated that their main reason for working flexibly was that their wife or partner works full time. A senior lecturer comments that *"it would be immoral to have two full time jobs with four million jobless."*

A letter from a Chief Technical Specialist, private sector reads: *"Where we live there is widespread unemployment. However, loss of benefits on taking a job mean that the only option is a full time job. On the other hand, once a family or household has one job and no longer receives benefits, part time work is an option for other family members. This results in 'work rich' households, sometimes to the detriment of family and social life, while other families are 'work poor'. My direct experience of this occurred recently when a community run cafe looked at employing a single mother. We discovered she would have to be paid £300 per week just to maintain her family income. This was beyond a full time post in the cafe, let alone the part time job she really wanted in order to look after her children properly.*

Current employment and benefit legislation result in part time work being a realistic option only for the already well off (or relatively well off) like myself. This is in part due to prevalent attitudes when the welfare state was established 50 years ago, but is insidiously reinforced by current political and moral attitudes, both on the right and the left. The failure of my then trade union to help me gain a part time position is a case in point.

I believe that the development of the social economy, which requires the freeing up of employment practices such as you advocate, is a way of making the 'market' work for communities, especially in economically poor areas such as where we live. I therefore welcome this opportunity to participate in developing new ways to work, and would welcome a further chance to be involved."

Quality of life

An improved quality of life, balancing all aspects of life: paid work, family and domestic commitments, community involvement, study and leisure was a desired aim of many men. A solicitor thinks that *"people wouldn't be working five days a week, they'd be working four days or less. I think people should have the same security of employment rights that they had as full time workers. Life is too short to be spending every single hour on work – men miss out on their children being brought up. I know people who work until 8 or 9pm every single night and they only see their children at weekends. They're missing out and are putting an unacceptable burden upon their partners, who are sometimes having to put three, sometimes four children to bed themselves".*

The general pace of life was seen as a problem. A trainer in the private sector said that *"I think why we're constantly having lots and lots of people who are having nervous breakdowns, and heart attacks and stress related illness is because of the pressure of work, or the pressure of life, and hairing down motorways".*

Increase in working from home

A number of men were already working partly from home and there was an awareness that this could increase in the future. One man working for a large private sector company suggests: *"As far as the future goes people should be able to do an enormous amount from home. There are reasons why you can't spend all your time at home because it's like shopping, you can shop by phone and computer, but it doesn't happen, because people like to go to the shops. People still need to interact. Offices provide that. I can never see people staying at home, not all the time. But I can see people doing one day a week, two days a week at home maybe. It does a number of other things, it saves on heating, it saves on energy, it saves on office space. You need to organise it properly. We are starting now to have shared desks for people, not just for working at home. Some of them have an office in this building, and an office in another building. They have an office which is shared between three or four people because it's unlikely that all three or four will be there at any one time. So you can convince people they can save money on office space, facilities, or services, meals, coffee, all these things. My ideal world is one where everyone in the country works three days a week. And I just can't see a way through to that."*

The future of work depends on a flexible response from employers. Some men want to work full time but not as a life sentence. Sabbaticals, unpaid periods of leave, flexitime, four day weeks are all very much on their agenda. But most of all, men enjoy their work more when they feel they have been able to make a choice about how and when they work.

Chapter eight:
Keeping pace with change

"An important element in any strategy for change is the provision of role models – individuals, families, workplaces, services and, indeed, societies where more equal sharing has been achieved or is being seriously worked towards."
Taken from *Men as Carers*

The days of lifelong, full time employment for men and women are over. Throughout the course of their lives, many adults will have to face periods without work or with part time work, and will have to be prepared to change constantly and adapt in the work which they do. Short term skills shortages can provide the initial incentive for organisations to become more family friendly. For example, the pharmaceutical industry is having to look very hard at ways to retain highly trained technical staff. Some employers then discover that they are meeting a more deep-seated demand amongst their own staff and potential employees for greater flexibility. Such flexibility makes the organisation better equipped to cope with peaks and troughs in demand, and the employer is able to cut down on overtime as a result as in the example provided by HM Treasury.

Organisational uncertainty

Different attitudes and approaches to work are emerging. For many years, individuals were not allowed or expected to bring any of their outside interests into the workplace. Men are starting to demand quality time along with taking a more equal role in family life. Yet work and family issues are still seen mainly as women's issues. Where 'family friendly' policies exist they are officially for men and women, but are used mostly by women. In order to change that companies need to explore specific strategies for adapting to fathers' new roles as well as mothers. The debate is shifting from family friendly policies to creating policies which take into account the needs of all employees. A way forward is to give men a voice as fathers within the workplace. Senior male managers who are interested in parenting are often in a position to effect change in the prevailing culture. Some of these men might be interested in more time with their own children, while others may be older men, who now regret their earlier inability to combine work and family responsibilities.

"Some of the older men that I've spoken to have said, that looking back on it they missed their children growing up because they were working at their career. So there's that regret."
Colin White

There is work to be done. Men want parental leave and paternity leave. Companies need to be convinced that father-friendliness might even help their profitability. An assessment of sickness and absence around birth might provide a useful analysis. Personnel departments can be instrumental in assessing needs.

In addition, more information is needed, both at organisational level and nationally. A range of research, both quantitative and qualitative would help, so that policy makers can better understand the individual arrangements within family structures. How do couples divide the work around care and raising children? Does the workplace support or hinder men who wish to assume a more equal share of family responsibilities? On such a basis of analysis and understanding a strategy can be established which balances 'top down' measures along with supporting existing informal arrangements and networks. For example, researchers in Norway have observed young Norwegian policemen negotiating hours with colleagues so they can collect children from day care centres.

Evaluation is only a starting point. The process of change will take a long time, running into decades. It has taken 20 years to reach the stage where nearly half of fathers takes some Parental Leave in Sweden. It is necessary for organisations to be prepared to listen, learn and respond flexibly to the needs of different people. Only in this way will they be able to create a truly diverse working environment within which they can gain the maximum potential from each individual.

Conclusions

The men in *Balanced Lives* were generous with time and information about their work and personal situations. Some might be embarrassed to be acknowledged as role models but their examples will provide a practical lead for organisations and men who are thinking about negotiating flexible arrangements. There is evidence that companies are not informed about what men want, and that men do not risk telling their employers about changing circumstances. This appears to be particularly true in the private sector. However, one man working for a company without any formal procedures for negotiating part time work stressed the importance of asking: *"My own experience is that if you make an approach, there are no organisational barriers to stop it happening."*

Lotte Bailyn, Professor of Management at the Massachusetts Institute of Technology is convinced that it is possible for American companies to meet simultaneously their productivity needs and the personal needs of their employees, and that to focus on only one of these critical concerns undermines the other. She argues that these are not peripheral issues that can be left to personnel assistants and counsellors. *"There is no escape from these problems; companies must include – explicitly, imaginatively, and effectively – the private needs of employees when re-engineering their work. Only if they do so can they gain a competitive edge."*

Men are negotiating and implementing changes in their lives, juggling priorities which include deep seated needs to care for children and to create more time to develop new skills and interests. One man could not say it better: *"I don't know of anybody on their deathbed who wished they had spent more time in the office whereas a lot wished they spent more time with their kids."* However, many organisations assume that male employees still live predominantly in traditional families rarely to be confronted with any family problems. Employers cannot afford to operate in a vacuum.

The reasons for working flexibly will change as technology further revolutionises work, and society changes. There is no doubt that organisations will continue to seek new and innovative ways of working. However, flexibility should not mean 'constant availability'. Employers and employees must jointly find ways to create a healthy balance between the needs of the organisation and the personal needs of individual employees.

Through the examples of innovation and good practice outlined in this book employers can actively review their policies and encourage men who would like to change their working arrangements. We also hope that the case histories will inspire those men who want to effect positive changes in their hours of work.

More and more men, like women, will work flexibly in the future. By doing this they will achieve more balanced lives. With action from both sides employers and employees can reap the benefits.

Chapter nine:
Achieving change

There are no easy solutions or standard ways of achieving change. So much depends on individual circumstances, the expectations and responsibilities within the job, the organisational culture and values, and current economic climate. If men are to be encouraged to share caring and domestic responsibilities for children and other family members, organisations need to acknowledge that fixed working hours and holidays are not enough to cover contingencies. Flexibility not only in time but also in working practices is the principle that underlies the following ideas to bring about change.

Individuals

♦ If you want to change your working arrangements, prepare yourself well, set out clear business objectives and ASK. It may be easier than you think.

♦ Find out if the organisation has an equal opportunities policy, flexible working practices, and whether policy is part of practice.

♦ Talk with other men who you think might be in a similar position or your staff or union representative for advice.

♦ Approach New Ways to Work for further information.

Organisations

Key issues in making flexible working a reality for men
Obtain support from the top for a culture where flexible working is seen as an option for all staff and where commitment equates with quality, high output and a balanced life, rather than with time spent at the workplace.

General
♦ Find out what employees want.

♦ Look at the age profile of your employees and anticipate change.

♦ Offer paid paternity leave and support for fathers.

♦ Offer parental leave.

♦ Provide role models from within the organisation.

♦ Encourage all staff to appreciate the benefits of flexible work patterns.

Communicating policies

When publicising flexible work policies, include examples of men using the schemes. State clearly that the options are aimed at men too. Use leaflets, posters, staff journals, staff guidelines, self-help groups.

Changing perceptions of the male model of work

Men in management, training or personnel posts could be given opportunities to explore myths and stereotypes, along with different communication patterns and styles of behaviour, by examining:

♦ how attitudes can change

♦ how their organisation reflects male values

♦ ways of achieving change within the organisation in both attitudes and behaviour

Monitoring and review

Acknowledge that developing more flexible work patterns will be a slow process and is part of a wider cultural change. For key points in achieving this see *Changing Times* published by New Ways to Work.

Government

Role models

Legislation can initiate and support change, but cannot always change attitudes. Positive role models are important. In Norway two Government Ministers took Parental Leave.

Paternity leave

Establish a statutory right, however limited, to paternity leave, of five days as recommended by the Employment Select Committee Report *Mothers in Employment*.

Parental leave

Adopt the following recommendation from the above Employment Committee Report:

"We recommend that the Employment Department initiate and publish research on the areas of the economy in which advances towards parental leave entitlement have been made, to reveal whether a voluntary approach to provision of parental leave is adequately benefiting women at work with dependent children. The research could also indicate the take-up level amongst employees and the costs imposed on employers as a result of parental leave. This information will then enable the Department to assess the impact of a statutory scheme of parental leave and the possibility of meeting the costs of a scheme from sources other than an increase in taxation or direct costs upon an employer."

Family leave

Introduce a minimum entitlement to family leave for all employees, of five days as recommended by the Employment Committee.

Pensions

Establish a review of both the pensions industry and the state pension scheme to establish that all people, regardless of the number of hours they work, are treated on an equitable basis and do not face unfair penalties.

Appendix:
The New Ways to Work survey

Background

Preliminary research

In 1994 Gill Forster, Senior Lecturer in Human Resource Management at Newcastle Business School, University of Northumbria, carried out a preliminary investigation in an attempt to identify answers to the following questions:

(a) What does the literature say about flexible working arrangements and men?

(b) What are the perceptions of men working flexibly with regard to how they are treated in the organisation, the issues and problems which arise from their working arrangements? Do they complement the literature?

Interviews took place with men working flexibly in three organisations within the Civil Service. An HRM representative was also interviewed to find out what was the actual policy for flexible working and how did it compare with the experiences of the male interviewees.

The literature review highlighted the following issues: organisations' lack of communication of policies, perceived lack of commitment, resistance from line managers, unequal treatment compared with full time workers, culture change and lack of career opportunities.

Methodology

Using the preliminary results as a basis for a questionnaire, this was first piloted with three men. In late 1994 New Ways to Work sent out a total of 85 questionnaires to men who were working on a flexible basis or had worked a flexible work option. The individuals were contacted in two ways. Some were known to be working flexibly by New Ways to Work at the beginning of the research. We were able to contact others through a letter in *Personnel Management*. Men also suggested contacting colleagues and friends who were working on a flexible basis.

New Ways to Work also contacted 141 employers in the public, private and voluntary sectors asking them to pass on questionnaires to men working flexibly at any grade within the organisation. Some of these employers were already known to offer flexible working to their employees. Others were approached because of their size and through an attempt to cover as many of the industrial and commercial sectors of the UK economy as possible. We found that men from these organisations were working in a variety of ways including job sharing, part time working, voluntary reduced hours and working from home.

The second half of the research involved in depth interviews with men who had completed the original questionnaire. We were not only interested in identifying men who were working as many flexible options as possible and in as wide a range of organisations as possible but also chose some respondents who had raised interesting questions which were not fully answered in the questionnaire. Ninety per cent of men indicated their willingness to be interviewed either on a confidential or named basis.

The results

The majority of men who replied to the survey are aged between 30-50. Men who are working flexibly are more likely to be found in skilled jobs in local authorities and the voluntary sector. In the private sector they are more likely to come from an older age group in order to phase into retirement. They work for multinational corporations and high street banks, voluntary organisations and small businesses. Although there is evidence of men working at all levels in organisations most men who replied work in middle to senior management. Forty per cent manage staff.

The types of jobs worked flexibly are extremely varied. The respondents include a solicitor, minister, landscape assistant, community alarm service operator, economic policy adviser, museum keeper, cycling officer, social worker, sub-editor on a national newspaper, GP/police surgeon, building surveyor, librarian, minerals monitoring assistant, pensions researcher, youth worker, lending officer, and mobile sheltered housing warden.

They work in London, Oxford, Hertfordshire, Birmingham, Sheffield, Leicester, Norwich, York, Milton Keynes, Edinburgh, Cheltenham,

Manchester, London, Boston, Chichester, Cambridge, Preston, Bath, Exeter, Brighton, Cheadle (Cheshire), Kendal (Cumbria).

Their reasons for working flexibly are very individual and according to circumstance. Some play a great part in rearing young children, others just want to be on hand to help with domestic responsibilities. Some have changed roles. Some participate in caring for grandchildren. Others use their time to pursue interests, consultancy work, and one to do police surgeon duties. Easing into retirement was a popular option.

Some men have achieved their ambitions while others consider the opportunity to work flexibly as a halfway house until their children are old enough for school or while they seek added qualifications. Most are very concerned by the financial implications and some have partners who are working full time to make flexible working viable. Some have called for greater flexibility within the particular flexible work options they work.

There is evidence of demand to work in whatever ways are needed to suit personal circumstances and views. Some are working flexibly because they do not have access to childcare or after school schemes, their organisations do not offer paternity leave or parental leave, and they use flexitime to ease the stress caused by the absence of such policies. Some have firmly chosen not to participate in the full time work culture because of high unemployment in their areas.

How long do they intend to work flexibly? Fifty one per cent of men surveyed replied 'foreseeable future' and fifteen per cent indicated between two and five years.

Summary tables

The following percentages are based on an analysis of 106 questionnaires.

Table 1: The options men worked

Job sharing	27%
Part time	39%
Voluntary reduced hours (V-time)	4%
Working from home	
(a) some of the time	7%
(b) all of the time	2%
Term time working	1%
More than 1 option	17%
Other	8%

NB Some people were working more than one option eg part time and from home and would appear in the statistics twice.

Table 2: The ages

Under 30	6%
30-39	33%
40-49	44%
50-59	15%
60 and over	2%

Table 3: The sectors

Local authority, Civil Service, Police	55%
Private sector	18%
Voluntary sector	9%
Education	8%
Health	6%
Other (Housing corporation, self employed, Church)	4%

Bibliography

Bailyn, L. (1993) **Breaking the Mold: Women, Men and Time in the Corporate World,** Free Press.

Carlsen, S. and Larsen, J.E. (1994) **The Equality Dilemma,** The Danish Equal Status Council.

Collinson, D. and Hearn, J. (1994) **Naming Men as Men: Implications for Work, Organisation and Management,** Gender Work and Organization, Volume 1, No 1, January.

Cooper, C.L. and Payne, R. (1988) **Causes, Coping and Consequences of Stress at Work,** John Wiley and Sons.

Cooper, C.L. and Lewis S. (1993) **The Workplace Revolution: Managing Today's Dual Career Families,** Kogan Page.

Curnow, B. and Fox, J.M. (1994) **Third Age Careers, Meeting the Corporate Challenge,** Gower.

Equal Opportunities Review (1994) **Paternity Leave,** May/June.

European Commission. (1994) **Employment in Europe.**

European Commission Network on Childcare and other Measures to Reconcile Employment and Family Responsibilities for Women and Men. (1993), **Men as Carers.**

Financial Times, 26.9.94

Haas, L. and Hwang P. **Fatherhood and Corporate Culture in Sweden,** unpublished paper.

Handy, C. (1989) **The Age of Unreason,** Arrow.

Handy, C. (1994) **The Empty Raincoat,** Hutchinson.

House of Commons Employment Committee, (1995) **Mothers in Employment,** Volume 1, HMSO.

International Labour Office. (1992) **Preventing Stress at Work,** Conditions of Work Digest, Volume 11, Number 2.

Kandola, R. and Fullerton, J. (1994) **Managing the Mosaic: Diversity in**

Action, Institute of Personnel and Development.

Labour Force Survey. (1994) Employment Gazette, July.

Lewis, S. and Cooper, C.L. (1987) **Stress in Dual-Earner Couples and Stage in the Life Cycle,** Journal of Occupational Psychology, 60, pp 289-303.

Martin, B. (1989) **Man about the House,** New Statesman and Society, 20th October, p. 28.

NHS Women's Unit (1994) **Creative Career Paths in the NHS; Report No 1 Top Managers.**

New Ways to Work (1993) **Changing Times: A Guide to Flexible Work Patterns for Human Resource Managers.**

New Ways to Work (1995) **Flexible Working in Local Government.**

OPCS (1990) **General Household Survey,** HMSO.

Population Trends, HMSO.

Quick, J.C., Nelson, D.J. and Quick, J.D. (1990) **Stress and Challenge at the Top: The Paradox of the Healthy Executive,** Wiley.

Rappoport, R. and Moss, P. **Men and Women as Equals at Work,** Occasional Paper No 11, Thomas Coram Research Unit.

Social Policy Research Findings No. 60, **Women's Pay and Family Income Inequality.**

Social Policy Research Findings No. 6, **More Work in Fewer Households.**

Social Trends, (1994), HMSO.

Trades Union Congress, (1995) **The Pros and Cons of Part Time Working: A TUC Survey,** February.

Vallance, I. (1994) **From Minor Sport to Major Force,** Personnel Management, September, p24.